Vincent van Gogh

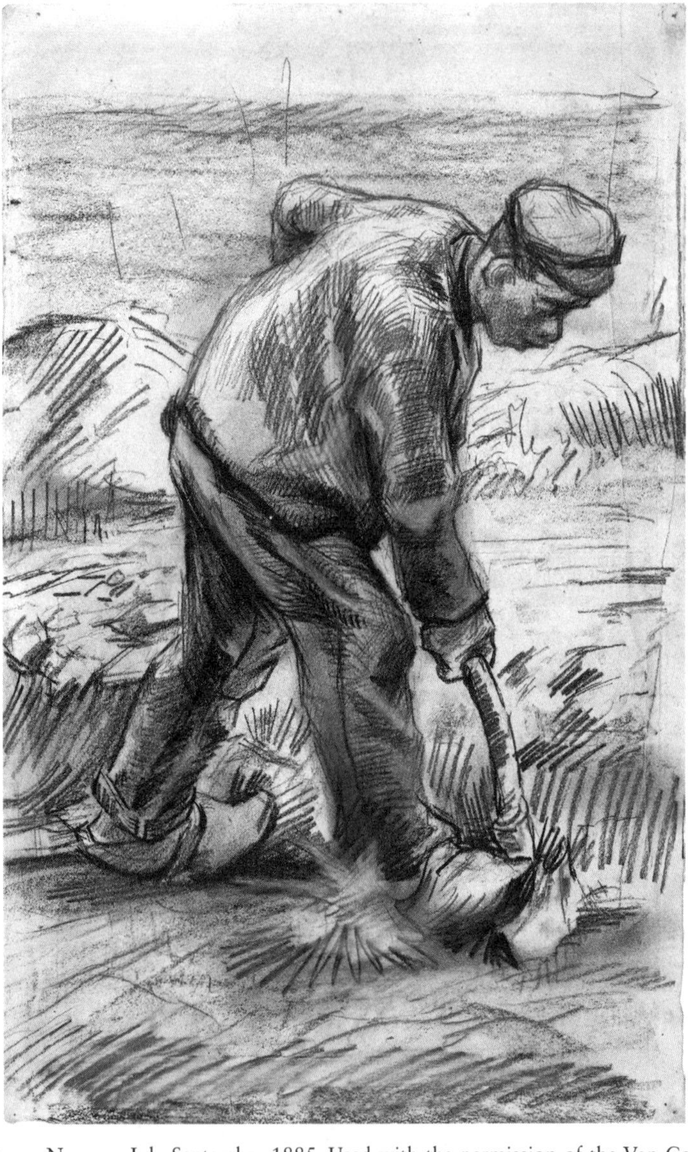

Digger. Nuenen: July-September 1885. Used with the permission of the Van Gogh Museum, Amsterdam (Vincent van Gogh Foundation).

MODERN SPIRITUAL MASTERS SERIES

Vincent van Gogh

His Spiritual Vision in Life and Art

CAROL BERRY

ORBIS BOOKS
Maryknoll, New York 10545

ORBIS BOOKS
Maryknoll, New York 10545

Fathers and Brothers MARYKNOLL

Founded in 1970, Orbis Books endeavors to publish works that enlighten the mind, nourish the spirit, and challenge the conscience. The publishing arm of the Maryknoll Fathers and Brothers, Orbis seeks to explore the global dimensions of the Christian faith and mission, to invite dialogue with diverse cultures and religious traditions, and to serve the cause of reconciliation and peace. The books published reflect the views of their authors and do not represent the official position of the Maryknoll Society. To learn more about Maryknoll and Orbis Books, please visit our website at www.maryknollsociety.org.

Published by Orbis Books, Box 302, Maryknoll, NY 10545-0302.

The letters of Vincent van Gogh cited in this volume have been translated by Carol Berry.

The letters of Vincent van Gogh are available in various editions, including:

The Complete Letters of Vincent van Gogh (3 volume set) (New York: Bullfinch Press, third edition, 2000); *Vincent van Gogh: The Letters: The Complete Illustrated and Annotated Edition* (6 volumes) (London: Thames and Hudson, 2009).

Manufactured in the United States of America

Library of Congress Cataloging-in-Publication Data
Berry, Carol (Art Educator)
Vincent van Gogh : his spiritual vision in life and art / Carol Berry.
pages cm. (Modern spiritual masters series)
ISBN 978-1-62698-152-2 (pbk.)
1. Gogh, Vincent van, 1853-1890—Criticism and interpretation. 2. Gogh, Vincent van, 1853-1890—Religion. I. Title.
N6953.G63B47 2015
759.9492—dc23 2015025470

Contents

Acknowledgments

Vincent van Gogh had always intrigued me. However, it wasn't until another great Dutchman, Fr. Henri Nouwen, taught a class at Yale Divinity School in 1979 called "The Compassion of Vincent van Gogh" that I began to study Vincent's life in earnest. What I found was a revelation of human compassion far exceeding my expectations. Here was a man who could fall on his knees before a flower, or a tree, or a vast field of wheat in adoration of their wonder and glory. Here was a man who sought with all his being to reveal his love for the Creator and for all of Creation. Henri Nouwen called Vincent his "saint" and invited his students to join him in studying the art and life of this artist who had touched him so deeply. I am indebted to Fr. Nouwen and to Sr. Sue Mosteller who, after Henri's death in 1996, sent me his class notes and urged me to "do something" with them.

I have benefited from reading many informative and sensitive works by others who have seen in Vincent van Gogh a remarkable human being. I am appreciative of the insights I could glean from them. Many of these books are listed in the bibliography. The main source, however, for my relationship with Vincent is the collection of his letters, originally written in Dutch and French, as well as the English translations.

I am deeply grateful to my husband, Steven, for his support and encouragement to devote my time to Vincent. I am equally grateful to my three sons, Andris, Mathias, and Kristof, and to my daughter-in-law Rahel, for being such willing listeners to my stories about this artist. They heard my lectures, read my manuscripts, offered wise insights, and shared my enthusiasm. And I am very grateful to Robert Ellsberg for having entrusted me with the writing of this book.

Carol Berry
Manchester, Vermont
July 2015

Introduction

Standing in front of a classroom of young art students I have sometimes asked them what they could tell me about the artist whose self-portrait I had displayed. Hands would fly up, vying for my attention. Before I could call on any one of them I would hear exclamations of "swirls in the sky," "sunflowers," "he cut off his ear." And many of the five- and six-year-olds knew this artist's name: Vincent van Gogh.

While in Sweden many years ago, my husband accompanied a pastor friend on a visit to a man who had recently lost his wife. As they entered the widower's simple apartment, my husband noticed a familiar image tacked to a wall. Between a few old photos of the man's family hung a cheaply framed calendar print of Vincent's sunflowers—a bright splash of color, beauty, and Van Gogh's comfort on a water-stained wall.

From kindergarten to college classrooms, from the business world to the art world, from the poor to the wealthy, from one end of the globe to the other, Vincent van Gogh is known for his "Starry Night" and his sunflowers. More than a century after his death, he remains in the forefront of the art world. Every year calendars and note cards of Vincent's most popular paintings are displayed and bought and their images cut out to be displayed on the walls of homes throughout the world.

Vincent grew up in a pastor's family. As an adolescent he entered into an apprenticeship with an art dealer but became disillusioned with the type of art he had to sell. He spent consecutive years searching for a vocation that would give meaning to his life and through which he could express the essence of his faith. He had an insatiable drive for knowledge, and he undertook intense soul-searching throughout his life to achieve greater understanding of the "Something on High"—the divine. Finally, after years of trial and failure and reduced to abject poverty and despair, he responded to an innate desire *to make sketches* and so devoted the last ten years of his life to the creation of art. His drawings and paintings flowed out of a deep well of life experience and a profound sense of compassion. Above all he loved nature. *If one truly loves nature, then one finds it beautiful everywhere* (London, April 30, 1874). In all aspects of nature and in his everyday human encounters Vincent came to see something worthy of art. He hoped to bring these ordinary things to the attention and appreciation of others. Finally, he was able to say:

> *I have found my work—I have something that I can live for with my heart and soul and which gives life inspiration and meaning. . . . I have a sure faith in art—a sure trust that it is a mighty current that will carry a person to a harbor—although he must do his bit too.*
>
> —The Hague, March 11, 1882

Vincent's "bit" demanded his all and the sacrifice of his personal desires. To pursue this calling, he depended on the full financial and moral support of his four-year younger brother Theo, who also gave his all so that Vincent could live and paint. Standing before any of Vincent's paintings one must never forget Theo's part in it. Vincent did not:

> *At the present time I don't find my paintings good enough yet based on the benefits I have received from you. But once they are good enough, I assure you that you have created them just as much as I, and that it is the two of us who have made them together.*
>
> —Arles, September 18, 1888

He also counted on Theo, who had become an art dealer, to promote and exhibit his paintings among the Impressionist artists in his Paris gallery. In this Theo had little success, at least in Vincent's lifetime; his paintings differed too greatly from popular tastes of the time. In the year of Vincent's death, however, a young art critic, Albert Aurier, who had come across some of his work, wrote a glowing report on Vincent van Gogh, highlighting the artist as a wounded, tortured genius, whose striking color contrasts and energetic lines expressed his personal suffering. In the critic's view, Vincent embodied the true artist, unabashed and driven, in touch with his creative self, unique and unattached to the conventions of his time. Thanks in part to Aurier's article in the *Mercure de France,* published in January 1890, the suns in Vincent's Provence paintings were beginning to rise above the art world of Paris and beyond. Vincent was uncomfortable with this praise, feeling that other artists were more deserving. Yet he did believe that one day his paintings would find friends among those who could appreciate the language of his art.

Just a few months after Vincent's sudden death that year, Theo succeeded in staging a small exhibition of Vincent's work, which attracted favorable attention from art critics and artists. But tragically, Theo himself died only a few months later. It was thanks to Theo's widow, who collected and saved all the rolled up canvasses and drawings stored in their cramped Paris apartment (against her brother's advice that she get rid of it all), that Vincent's work survived. Returning to her native Holland she began the arduous task of cataloguing and framing and, with the help of artist friends, exhibiting and lending Vincent's work to museums and collectors. It is from her house in a small Dutch town that the popularization of Vincent's work truly began. Within twenty years of his death, his reputation emerged from obscurity to achieve worldwide recognition. Since then his paintings have traveled the globe, and today they command bids of millions of dollars at world-class auctions. It is hard to imagine how Vincent would deal with this attention and acclaim.

Vincent wanted his work to sell one day, but not for much. He expressly wanted poor people to be able to hang cheerful pictures on the walls of their miserable homes. All he hoped was that his art would speak and touch some people in comforting ways. He wanted to be good for something and to give something to the world in gratitude for his existence.

> *The world concerns me only so far in that I feel a certain obligation and duty, as it were, because I have walked around this world for 30 years—to leave a certain souvenir in the form of drawings, or paintings, out of gratitude. Not made to please this or that art movement, but in which an honest human feeling is expressed.*
>
> —Nuenen, mid-June 1884

What is it that draws the multitudes to museums in many parts of the world to stand before his "Potato Eaters," his "Starry Night," and his wheat fields swaying under the southern sun? Is Vincent's work comforting? During a lecture many years ago about Vincent van Gogh, I projected his painting of a pair of very well-worn work shoes onto the screen. One older lady couldn't help exclaiming that this painting especially, more than the sunflowers, wheat fields, or human portraits, spoke to her. Interrupting my talk, I asked her to explain her feelings. While looking intently at the slide, she quietly said, "Oh, but I can't explain. This image just moves me." She paused, and then added, "It touches me deeply." Such a response to Vincent's paintings is not unusual. People are drawn to Vincent's art but can't quite explain why. When Vincent painted the still life of worn work boots, he said that he didn't need to paint a face to portray the human emotions of sadness and suffering. These could be conveyed just as well, or maybe even more vividly, through a pair of well-worn shoes. These shoes, like many of his paintings, communicate what Vincent called "an honest human feeling." Expressing human emotions that are personal and universal at the same time, such paintings do touch and can, in a mysterious way, comfort people.

In addition to the expressive quality of Vincent's work, there is the lure of a man whose life ended in tragedy, who suffered from loneliness and depression, who painted as if his life depended on it—which it did. Thanks to the legacy of his over eight hundred letters we know much about Vincent the man. The visible brush strokes in his paintings, like tracks in soft soil, make his presence palpable, and we stand before his paintings engaged in a visual dialogue directed at the viewer. We are drawn in and moved by his animated lines and his bold colors. Vincent touches something in us; he hits a common chord. He is a wounded healer who articulates through his language of art the authenticity of the human condition. Vincent didn't intend for us to analyze his art or our reactions to it. He wanted us to reverberate with his enthusiasm and empathy, and with his love for the subjects he painted.

Much has been written about Vincent based on psychological models and materialistic worldviews. Yet Vincent embraced an integral worldview, a view affirming that the divine Spirit—the "Something on High"—is at the core of everything, both within and without. Once he began to paint he dropped all religious language and abandoned institutionalized religion. But he remained deeply spiritual. In today's largely materialistic and analytical society, Vincent has been misunderstood and misinterpreted by those who do not integrate the spiritual with the material. Vincent's eccentricities have been looked upon as madness-induced. The focus has often been on signs of mental imbalance. And yet the essence of his correspondence and of his paintings speaks otherwise. If Vincent's life is looked upon as a whole—his life story, his paintings, and his letters—we see a human being on a spiritual quest, longing to understand his place and purpose in divine creation. Serving God and becoming like Jesus were essential to his quest. Most critical analysis of his psychological "fitness" falls short when his passion for God and his desire to minister and to care are not placed as the central and driving motivation for all he sought to be and do—and paint.

In this book I present Vincent van Gogh as a man whose art expressed a deeply spiritual vision. His strong desire was to minister, to comfort, to help people enter into solidarity with a suffering and searching humanity. Vincent believed that as a painter he had the duty to paint the essence of life, making visible that which is invisible. Twentieth-century artists echoed this belief as the definition of art's purpose. He believed that painters understood the natural world and could teach others to see and to love this world, and ultimately to see through the present reality to the creative spirit animating it all.

In these pages I attempt to clarify the often-missed spiritual dimension that was the driving force in Vincent's life. He hoped his paintings would move us to see our common bond as part of God's creation. As we enter into his world of devotion and service we may discover him as one of the great spiritual guides of our time.

Part I

Life Is a Sowing Time

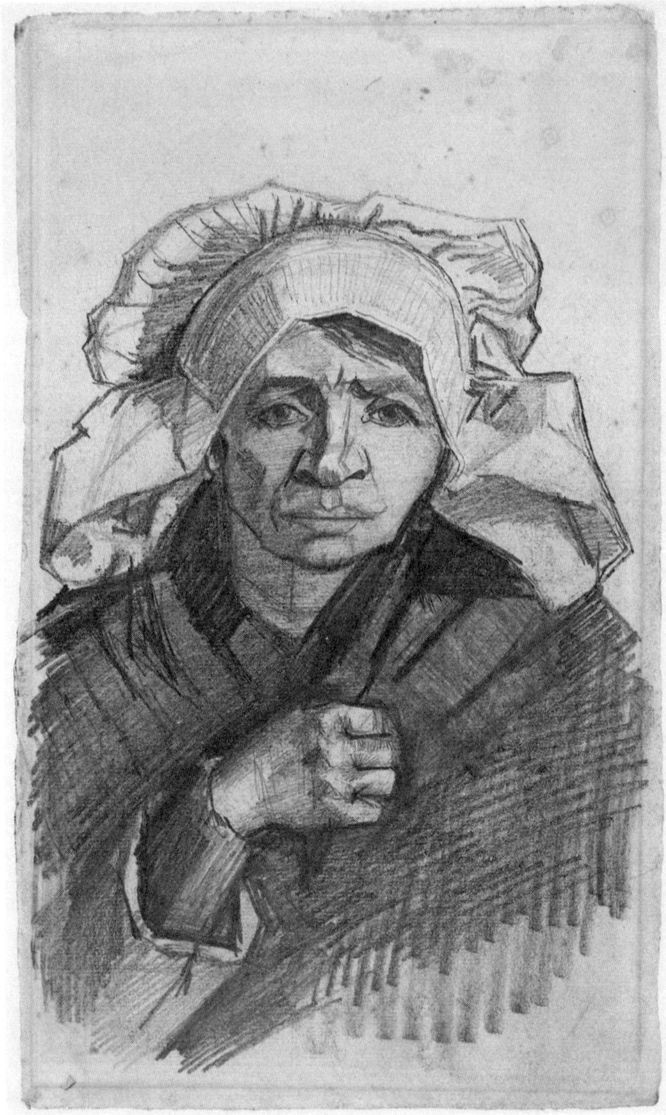

Head of a Woman. Nuenen: December-May, 1884-85. Used with permission of the Van Gogh Museum, Amsterdam (Vincent van Gogh Foundation).

1

The Country Boy from Brabant

One begins to see clearly that life is only a kind of sowing time, and the harvest is not here.

—The Hague, February 8, 1883

The painter of golden wheat fields, cobalt blue skies, radiant sunflowers, and brilliant suns began his life in the cold and wet climate of the north. During his childhood in a Dutch village of rural Brabant the seeds were sown that would one day ripen into a life of passionate creativity. Future trials and errors in search for his "raison d'être" contributed to the forceful vitality of the art he created during the last ten years of his life. Despite the lack of recognition while he lived, Vincent van Gogh felt that his paintings would one day speak to people who had a heart and mind to understand. *If I should accomplish in putting some warmth and love into my work, it will find its friends. . . . To keep on working is the thing* (The Hague, on or about April 2, 1883). Today Vincent's paintings have found their friends—the harvesters of an art legacy imbued with a creative force that had its beginnings in the Brabant village of Zundert over one hundred fifty years ago.

A CHILDHOOD ROOTED IN THE PARABLES OF JESUS

I am so entirely captivated by that figure [the Sower].

—Cuesmes, September 7, 1880

On March 30, 1853, Vincent Willem van Gogh was born in Zundert, a sleepy little town surrounded by swamps, wind-swept heath, and vast treeless expanses of meadows. Vincent was his parents' second-born child. His birth followed the death of a brother, also named Vincent Willem, born a year earlier on the same day but who died soon after his birth. For years Vincent walked by the cemetery of his father's church seeing the grave marked with his own name and birth date as a constant reminder of the child he had replaced. Years later Vincent indicated that he had been deprived of a close affectionate relationship with his mother who had conceived him while in mourning for her first son. His parents had five more children, two boys and three girls. Vincent became especially close to his brother Theo, four years his junior.

Vincent and his siblings grew up in a parsonage. Their father was a Calvinist pastor whose strict adherence to his faith left a lasting impression on all of his children. Many of the Calvinist tenets shaped Vincent's faith journey, especially the admonition to strive for an understanding of his divine calling through a constant discipline of self-education. In order to know God one had to know one's self. The arts and sciences and the "Book of Nature" were paths that could lead to self-knowledge. According to Calvin, everything from a blade of grass, to the colorful flowers, the mighty trees and tall mountains, was intended to instill reverence and joy. And Vincent did rejoice in all he saw, from the creeping insects, to birds' nests, to the puddles reflecting the muted colors of the sky. Above all, Vincent learned that the essence of his Christian faith was to be found in the person of Jesus, the carpenter of Nazareth. The Gospels of the New Testament revealed that this simple laborer was the incarnation of the divine, the Christ, who used parables to help the people of his time understand that they too were filled with God's indwelling spirit.

Vincent and his siblings grew up hearing the stories of Jesus told by their father. Many parables used imagery that mirrored the daily rhythms of rural life taking place in the meadows surrounding Zundert. The story of the Sower sowing his seeds, as the symbol for the spreading of the Word of God, was one that was often repeated. Vincent was familiar with the sight of actual sowers plodding along the ploughed furrows, strewing their seeds every spring. Sowers, harvesters, gleaners, and diggers populated the landscapes of Vincent's youth. He watched the stooped figures of peasants planting and digging up potatoes. He heard the sharp sounds of ploughs cutting through the earth and inhaled the scent of the freshly cut hay. These were sensual experiences that became as much a part of him as the parables of Jesus he listened to while sitting by the hearth in the parsonage. Vincent developed an intimate relationship with nature and with the people whose lives were intricately woven into its fabric. Years later, sowers and reapers continued their cyclical labor on his canvases as parables in paint. Learning that the biblical stories and images were embedded in rural life reinforced the Calvinist premise that God spoke through creation. "In the beginning was the Word and the Word was with God, and the Word was God" (John 1:1). "Jesus was the Word made flesh. The Word of life and light" (John 1:2-5; 14). This was consistent with the Reformers' belief that to hear God and discern God's voice was humanity's highest calling. Knowledge of God, the Reformers believed, was summed up by the Apostle Paul who insisted, "Faith comes by hearing, and hearing by the Word of God" (Romans 10:17). Vincent was therefore influenced first by the Bible stories told within the family circle, which were reinforced in the church where his father preached. He was equally influenced by his experience of hearing nature speak to him. The Reformers thought of God as a "speaking God" (*Deus loguens*). At an early age Vincent sought to listen.

ROOTED IN THE SOIL OF THE BRABANT

I hope there will always be something of the Brabant fields and heath in us, which years of city life will not be able to remove, especially because art renews and strengthens it.

—The Hague, November 16 or 17, 1882

He often escaped the confines and rigorous routines of the parsonage to roam the enormous silence of the heath under the wide vault of heaven, where insipient rain, cool winds, or the warming rays of the northern sun affected his moods. Vincent's imagination was fed by the Dutch landscape with its far-off horizon circling around him, interrupted here and there by the church steeple of a distant village. Such a scene made its way onto canvas toward the end of his life while living in the south of France and homesick for the north. "Starry Night" was painted from the memory of countless walks as the *twilight was falling, on one side the sky was still aglow from the setting sun, on the other, the moon was rising,* or, as he related, walking through a meadow with trees and houses on the horizon, *over which the church spire rises* and seeing in the distance *the lamps lit in the village.* In "Starry Night" these familiar scenes are nestled among the wavy hills and flaming cypresses of Provence. And above village and church the sky sounds with vibrating spirals and pulsating stars. And it is as if *all nature seems to speak . . . Nature or God does it for everyone who has eyes and ears and a heart to understand* (The Hague, November 26 and 27, 1882). The natural world instilled Vincent with a reverence for something greater than himself. He looked to the stars in the night sky—to the "Something on High"—as a source of faith and hope, comfort and inspiration. Below his feet the fertile soil of rural Brabant nurtured the roots of his very being. His sister commented to a biographer, "Nature spoke to Vincent with a thousand voices and his soul listened." Indeed, Vincent learned to experience life not as a set of rules, but as a series of sacred chords, individually striking his soul. All the impressions he gathered on the heath as a boy touched his innermost core and remained forever imprinted in his memory. These impressions were to give him solace in times of loneliness, feeding the creative work of his later years:

> *Many landscape painters don't have that intimate knowledge of nature which those have who looked with sentiment at the fields from childhood on. . . . You will say, but everyone has surely seen landscapes and figures since they were children. Question: Was everyone also thoughtful as a child? Question: Did everyone who saw them—heath, grassland, fields, woods—also love them, and the snow and the rain and the storm? Not everyone has done that the way you and I have; it takes a special kind of environment and circumstances that have to contribute to it, and also a particular kind of temperament and character to make it take root.*
>
> —The Hague, between December 4 and 9, 1882

Separated from the larger outdoors was his mother's parsonage garden. Here Vincent and his siblings could closely observe the yearly life cycles: from the sowing of seeds, to the care of seedlings and the picking and harvesting of blossoms and fruit. Their mother who loved to draw flowers and believed in their symbolic value passed this passion on to her children. A violet was not just a pretty flower but it signified faithfulness and humility; an apple would call to mind the story in Genesis of Adam tempted by Eve; and sunflowers bloomed to instill the sense of adoration and gratitude. All this schooling in nature studies created in Vincent a love for symbols and metaphors. Many of them found expression in paint years later.

ROOTED IN A FAMILY OF A DIFFERENT KIND

> *We have our roots in a different kind of family life after all.*
>
> —The Hague, November 24, 1882

The daily customs and habits modeled and taught by their parents strongly shaped Vincent's and his siblings' personalities and outlook on life. Throughout his life Vincent remained mindful that his family was different from most and that much of what he did and felt was a result of his parsonage upbringing. Some of his parents' admonitions and values he wholeheartedly embraced, while others sparked his rebellion. A very strong influence on Vincent was the great emphasis placed upon doing one's duty, upon being decent, dependable, and solid. In many of the letters he wrote over the years he would reflect on what constituted his duty. Once he started to draw he believed that *one must not count on selling one's drawings, yet it is one's duty to make them in such a way that they have a certain value and are serious . . .* (The Hague, November 5, 1882). And it was *one's duty to try to do the right thing, even though one cannot go through life without making mistakes, without having regrets or sorrow. Somewhere I read, "Some good must come by clinging to the right"* (The Hague, between December 13 and 18, 1882). When he began to paint, Vincent repeatedly expressed that it was his duty to put honest sentiments into his work so that his art would elicit serious thoughts and emotions in his viewers. Doing one's duty meant one couldn't be idle. Idleness was considered sinful; it was imperative to engage in useful and lucrative endeavors. Vincent tried to live up to his familial expectations through many future trials and failures. In terms of his family's criteria, he never achieved the respectability demanded of the Van Gogh name. Nevertheless, the value of being duty-bound and hard-working remained deeply embedded.

Among the traits his parents tried to instill in their children, but that Vincent rejected, was class-consciousness. Vincent's parents put great stock in upholding the Van Gogh name through right behavior and respectable careers. The Van Gogh children were to associate with well-to-do, decent companions; they were discouraged from interacting with the village children or with peasant families. At that time the role and standing of the pastor demanded a certain distance from his parishioners. The social obligations of a pastor would later create a conflict for Vincent. He would discover that the "role" of pastor, the "office" of clergyman, and the institutional construct of religion created a barrier preventing a pastor from truly following Jesus. As a young man, away from home, Vincent rejected this class distinction. Yet, Pastor Van Gogh and his wife did fulfill their call of ministering to their parishioners. Vincent witnessed many of his parents' acts of kindness and generosity. As a young boy he sometimes accompanied his father on pastoral visits into the homes of poor or sick peasants. In their simple cottages he could perceive their basic human needs firsthand. Here among the rural poor, Vincent learned very early to feel empathy and compassion for people who suffered.

> *Even as a boy I sometimes looked up with endless sympathy and respect into a half-withered female face where it was written, as it were: life and reality have left its mark there.*
>
> —Etten, on or about December 23, 1881

Thirty years later he painted portraits of people with such faces as "Saints" (Saint-Rémy, September 10, 1889). His future drawings and paintings of weavers, potato eaters, and the poor he encountered in charitable homes reflect his strongly felt kinship with peasants and common laborers upon whom everyone in society depends. Thanks to him, their likenesses hang alongside portraits of the wealthy in art museums around the world.

The family unit was touted to the Van Gogh children as the most important nucleus of their lives and, for Vincent and his siblings, this resulted in a lifelong loyalty to one another. The parental home was always the ultimate refuge and the filial bonds between the siblings remained strong no matter where life took them in their adult years. Letter writing became the main vehicle to maintain and strengthen the ties between them, to encourage, uphold, and advise. Many of the virtues exemplified and instilled by Vincent's parents are discussed in his letters, some critically, others in admiration and gratitude. He wrote to his younger brother Theo that they couldn't help the way they were since their early parsonage upbringing always remained a part of them.

Vincent's life changed drastically at the age of eleven when he was sent away to a boarding school, effectively ending his childhood freedom to roam and explore his beloved heath. The homesickness he suffered from being forced into the cold environment of an institution for the next four years and his perception of being unwanted and rejected by his family deeply affected him. He had already suffered from a deficiency in a close mother-son relationship that had left him feeling inferior and hypersensitive. This sensitivity continued to undermine his self-confidence and contributed to recurring bouts of deep sadness that in later years turned into depression. At the root of Vincent's sorrow, was a yearning for love, acceptance, and affirmation. His low self-esteem was aggravated and enhanced by the high expectations everyone had for him to "be someone" respectable and well-positioned.

ROOTED IN THE LANGUAGE OF PICTURES

> [A work of art], *as long as it is well understood, can move one more deeply than one may be aware.*
>
> —Amsterdam, March 3, 1878

Long before Vincent picked up a reed pen with the intention of learning the skills of an artist, he was already looking at the world with an artist's eye. He practiced his observation skills largely during his long jaunts through the Brabant landscape. But another influence on his visual acuity derived from a verbal-pictorial teaching method popular in Northern Europe at the time. It was believed that images could foster a greater understanding of hard-to-explain concepts. This manner of teaching had its origins in the sixteenth and seventeenth centuries and came to be called the Northern Emblematic Tradition. It claimed that the observed was imbued with metaphorical and symbolical meanings; ordinary objects or scenes, whether in nature or in pictures, could be used to point to desired ethical and moral values, character traits, and truths. To instill the proper values, children were often surrounded by art prints in their homes.

There were three prints hanging in Vincent's father's study that had a lasting impact on the young boy who looked at everything with such serious intensity. One of these prints showing an older man tenderly embracing a youth, was entitled "The Return of the Prodigal Son," by Ary Scheffer. Based on the New Testament parable of the same name (Luke 15:11-32), it depicted the moment when the father embraced his wayward son who returned home an utter failure after having squandered all his inheritance. Another image was a print based on an artwork by Jacobus Van der Maaten called "The Harvest." It showed a funerary procession through a field of ripe corn where the reapers paused from their harvesting to pay respect to a somber group of people passing by. Against a bright sky, the silhouette of a church steeple beckoned the black clad people processing there. It was an image of the real harvest of corn, as well as the reminder of human mortality—the harvest of a human soul. The third image was an etching of a baby's cradle by Rembrandt. A mystical light in an otherwise very dark chamber illuminated the infant within the cradle. All three of the pictures that hung in Pastor Van Gogh's study contained scenes with narratives that evoked strong emotions. Through such images, Vincent had been taught to see that the ordinary moments of life were indicators of deeper meanings beyond what was observable. Each of the storied images became interwoven with Vincent's own life.

The image of "The Prodigal Son" was particularly prophetic for Vincent, who would become such a wandering son, always returning home to his parents after failed attempts to "make it" in the world. He would forever yearn for that welcoming and accepting fatherly embrace depicted so tenderly by the artist. The image and its biblical message of a heavenly Father's unconditional embrace continued to give Vincent hope once he left his parental home.

The theme of "The Harvest," which also came to be called "Funeral Procession through the Corn Field," would figure often in Vincent's future paintings. Fields of wheat and corn in all their stages of growth always took on metaphorical overtones, associated with humanity in all the cycles of death, growth, ripening, and the promise of rebirth. He continued to take comfort in his walks through fields of growing grain. Looking at the fields and painting them would one day make him feel a sense of belonging to a larger whole. Writing to his sister years later, after having painted many fields of wheat, Vincent exclaimed, *I, who have neither wife nor child, have the need of seeing the wheat fields* (Saint-Rémy, July 2, 1889).

The simple image of a cradle by Rembrandt was a symbol of the biblical nativity, of vulnerability, of love and nurture, of being safe in the embrace of parental care. It was meant to evoke the emotions one feels when thinking of the nucleus of a family. In years to come, the sight of a cradle, of babies and mothers, always moved Vincent, filling him with a sense of yearning for something that was missing in his life. When he was older, Vincent saw other works by Rembrandt in the museums he visited. Rembrandt's ability to tell biblical stories without words touched Vincent deeply. It was Rembrandt who would one day provide the decisive affirmation for Vincent to turn to art as his expressive language. The image of a child surrounded by an otherworldly light could have been in Vincent's thoughts when he wrote years later, with a cradle and a newborn child by his side:

> *If one feels the need of something great, something infinite, something where one feels one can see God, one need not go far to find it. I think I saw something deeper, more eternal than the ocean, expressed in the eyes of a little baby when it awoke in the morning.*
>
> —The Hague, December 10, 1882

In the last two years of his life, the subject of a cradle reappeared in the painting called "La Berceuse" (The Cradle Rocker): a portrait of a real mother holding the end of a rope that rocks the invisible cradle of her newborn child. It was a painting that was intended to hang in sea-faring vessels so that sailors would feel comforted during their long absences on stormy seas—by remembering their mothers rocking them to sleep.

Vincent's creative imagination had thus been fed at an early age by his environment and parental upbringing. Everything that young Vincent took into himself during his formative years remained very present to him. After leaving home to live in cities, he added the pictures seen in galleries and museums and the stories read in hundreds of books into his ever-expanding treasury of images and memories. The biblical parables served as templates for his ability to see beyond the narrated events of a story to the interpretation of a larger truth. He never lost the conditioned skill of associating an image with a concept or story, linking one thing with another, layering meanings upon meanings, stories upon images, and images upon stories.

FOREVER A COUNTRY BOY AT HEART

> *Feeling, even a sensitive feeling, for the beauties of nature is not the same as a religious feeling, even though I believe they are connected. It is the same as with a*

> *feeling for art. Almost everybody has some feeling for nature—but there are only a few who feel that God is Spirit and those who worship Him must worship in spirit and in truth.*
>
> —Paris, September 17, 1875

Throughout his adult life when anxiety threatened to overcome him, Vincent returned in memory to this childhood years in Zundert. The mere thoughts of the places where he and his brother Theo had shared a brotherly intimacy brought him solace. Suffering from loneliness in the last year of his life, he sought comforting reassurance by painting the image of a bedroom. While modeled on the bedroom of the little house he had occupied in Arles, the walls were painted blue, reminiscent of his bedroom in the Zundert parsonage. Such a concrete expression of his memory calmed him in times of turmoil and provided his mind with a tangible place of rest. He intended this painting to be a place of refuge for anyone looking at it in the future.

All the "roots" of his childhood years were crucial in shaping Vincent's future path as an artist. His recollections of the Zundert landscape reinforced his lifelong attachment to nature and to rural landscapes anywhere. He always felt grounded by remembering the windswept heath of his youth or years later by looking at a wheat field swaying in the mistral wind of the Provence—and by seeing any of this even in the form of a painting. He never lost his sense of belonging to the soil or to its laborers. The figures of sowers and reapers, the fertile fields, pollard willows, country roads, and cloudy skies of the Brabant landscape appeared again and again in his drawings and eventually were transformed by colors and emphatic brush strokes in his paintings done in the south of France. The "Book of Nature" was always the source for paintings. In his core he remained the country boy of the Brabant—a boy who would shed the Van Gogh name in the future and simply become "Vincent."

The love of art and literature, of writing letters, of the compassionate outreach toward one's neighbor, and the belief that God's presence was in every blade of grass, all these elements in his life were a lasting gift Vincent's parents had bestowed upon him. They set him on a trajectory of learning and searching that deepened and widened his knowledge and wisdom and faith. His soul listened, and he eventually responded.

2

Immersion into the World of Art

There is so much that is beautiful in art, if only one can remember what one has seen, one is never empty or completely lonely, and never alone.

—Etten, on or about November 13, 15, or 16, 1878

ART DEALER'S APPRENTICE

Admire [art] *as much as you can; most people do not admire enough. . . . Always take many walks and keep your love of nature, for that is the true way to learn to understand art more and more. Painters understand nature and love her and teach us to see her.*

—London, beginning of January, 1874

The four years Vincent spent in boarding schools were overshadowed by the sense of banishment from the parsonage. At the age of fifteen his parents sent him away again to learn the trade of an art dealer. Two of his uncles had ties with the printing and art dealership firm Goupil & Cie., which had branches in several cities. The boy of the windswept heaths and wide horizons was to spend the next nine years in the narrow alleys and urban landscapes of The Hague, London, and Paris. In these cities he was drawn to the laboring classes and the poor, seeing in them the same kinds of struggle he had witnessed among the peasants in the thatched roof cottages and potato fields of the Brabant. Vincent's empathy for the suffering of humankind led him to live in solidarity among those who struggled the hardest.

During the first few years of his apprenticeship, he was propelled by his sense of duty into an ardent commitment to do well in the profession chosen for him. Goupil & Cie. was renowned for selling printed reproductions of famous artworks, catering to an increasingly art conscious middle class. Copying original works of art, gallery artists created printing plates from which many copies could be made and sold, thus making art prints an affordable commodity. Captivated as Vincent was by storied images, the pictures hanging on the walls of the Goupil galleries provided plenty of opportunities to ponder and interpret their meaning. Vincent and Theo (a future art dealer himself) eventually had large collections of such prints that they traded with one another and their artist friends. Descriptions and lists of them abound in their future correspondence.

With the same sense of adventure and excitement that had led Vincent to look for birds' nests in the hedges and high grasses around Zundert, he spent his free time exploring the cities' museums and galleries. He read and acquired as much knowledge as he could about artists' lives and their styles of art. He absorbed the stories told through their canvases as intensely as he had listened to the biblical stories as a child. His discovery of the artist Jean-Francois Millet, in whose pastoral paintings he recognized the peasants he had seen laboring in the Brabant fields of his youth, filled him with enthusiasm. Upon seeing the image of a farmer and his wife pausing to pray while standing in their field—"The Angelus"—Vincent wrote enthusiastically to Theo, *That is it—that is rich, that is poetry* (beginning of January, 1874). He would go so far as to say that the places where Millet was exhibited were "holy ground" (Paris, June 29, 1875). While Millet idealized the arduous life of the peasants in his paintings, he also succeeded in bringing these marginalized people into the awareness of the art-viewing public. Vincent's collection of many prints of Millet's rural paintings would become highly instrumental in guiding his own early attempts at drawing. Such prints by Millet and other artists he admired would be tacked to the walls of all the places where he lived. As long as he was surrounded by art, he was never completely alone, for the pictures spoke to him. And he in turn filled his future letters with evaluations of the artists he admired and descriptions of their art. He often compared the scenes of cityscapes or the fields and forests he walked through and the sensations they caused within him to specific artworks he had seen in the city's galleries and museums. Describing the experience of a walk he took with some friends he wrote:

> *We walked along the Buitenkant and there by the sandworks at the Oosterspoor, I can't tell you how beautiful it was in the twilight. Rembrandt, Michel and others have painted it, the ground dark, the air still lit by the glow of the setting sun, the row of houses and towers visible above, everywhere the lights in the windows, everything being reflected in the water. And the people and carriages like small black figures everywhere. Just as one sometimes sees in a Rembrandt. And it affected us so that we began talking about all sorts of things.*
>
> —Amsterdam, June 4 and 5, 1877

THE RIJSWIJK WALK

> *How I should like to have you here. That Rijswijk walk holds memories for me that are perhaps the most beautiful I have. If we speak again, maybe we shall talk about them again.*
>
> —London, July 20, 1873

> *I very often think of that walk on the Rijswijk road, when we drank milk together at the mill there after the rain.* —Cuesmes, between June 22 and 24, 1880

Walking was something Vincent did a lot, often alone. It was an active, purposeful walking—a means of getting from place to place at no cost, and a time to think, to observe, and to discover the scenes that inspired the artists he admired. *Everything there makes one think of Rembrandt's etchings* (Amsterdam, May 19, 1877). Both Theo and Vincent habitually went for long walks whenever they were together, enjoying the scenery, the exercise, but even more so the chance to talk "about all sorts of things" since the moods created by the art-inspiring views somehow enabled them to talk more freely and more intimately. It was on one of these early communal walks that the bond between the two teenage brothers was forged. This bond led to one of the most formidable and copious letter exchanges in art history and an art partnership without which there wouldn't have been a "Starry Night," or the popular prints of sunflowers to hang in our homes.

Theo came to visit his brother while Vincent was apprenticing at the branch of Goupil & Cie. in The Hague. They took a long stroll together along the canal in an area of the city called Rijswijk. When a sudden rainstorm took them by surprise they found shelter in a nearby mill. While waiting out the storm the miller offered them a drink of fresh milk. Sitting together enjoying their milk the two brothers had a chance to talk intensely, honestly, and intimately with each other. Away from their childhood home and not having spent much time together in the last few years, they may have experienced a sense of wonder at discovering each other as young men. Their talk was uncensored, uninterrupted, and not watched over by strict parents and nosy siblings. They had always been brothers, but now, as they sat in the shelter of the mill, they became friends and soul mates. As they left that Rijswijk mill they vowed never to lose the close and intimate relationship they felt at that moment. After Theo returned to Zundert, Vincent wrote him his first letter. In the ensuing years there were over 650 more to follow, first written in Dutch, then in French. One of the letters written several years after their walk refers to this special time they spent together, as would other letters over the years:

> *I also say once again that I long for you so much, isolated from everything, because I need sympathy and warmth. I would so much like to take a walk with you again—even though the Rijswijk mill is not there anymore.*
>
> —The Hague, July 19, 1882

In years to come, amidst the storms of life, Vincent never forgot intensely emotional and intimate moments in whose memory he found refuge.

DEFINING THE MISSION OF ART

> [I hope] *that you find things there that will stimulate you and that will provide good food for your inner life. For this is what great art does, and those are the works by them who apply themselves heart, mind, and soul . . . whose words and deeds are full of spirit and life.* —Etten, July 22, 1878

As an apprentice art dealer Vincent had to learn as much as he could about the art he was trained to sell. His great hunger for learning drove him to seek out the art displayed in museums and other galleries and to read any available books about the lives of artists. The more he learned and observed, the more he developed his own views and interests. The art hanging on the walls of the Goupil galleries at the time was traditional and done by artists who adhered to the rules set forth by the art academies—portraits, mythological and biblical scenes, exotic places. Beyond the walls of Goupil, Vincent encountered the art of a younger generation of artists seeking to break out of institutional restraints.

Art by contemporary artists of The Hague School highlighted the Dutch landscape in fresh colors and spontaneous scenes of ordinary life. As Vincent looked at their renderings of Dutch city streets and pastoral landscapes, he felt the same strong sensations he experienced on his walks through The Hague or the fields beyond.

Vincent found that the French realist painters whose subjects were the peasants, the laborers, and the cities' poor, succeeded in eliciting in him the same strong feelings of empathy he felt when encountering them in real life.

British illustrators whose work he admired in the periodical *The Graphic* were masters at creating honest images of the destitute in public almshouses and soup kitchens. Theirs was an art that spoke about the reality of poverty he had witnessed himself; it was an art that addressed the present-day conditions in the streets of large cities. These realist artists hoped to use such images to bring about an awareness among the reading and viewing public that would eventually lead to social change. They were the social activists of their day, rallying to improve the living conditions for the city's factory workers.

Vincent felt strongly that in these paintings and illustrations the role of art and religion could share the same concern and aim—to ease the hardships of the poor and recognize their worth and dignity. Vincent felt that art made for the people *is the highest, noblest calling for any artist* (The Hague, November 1, 1882):

> *What I appreciate in Herkomer, Fildes, Holl and the other founders of* The Graphic, *why they still mean more to me . . . and will continue to, is that they chose subjects which . . . have something noble and where a more serious sentiment is expressed. That especially must remain, I think. An artist need not be a clergyman or a*

> *churchwarden, but must certainly have a warm heart for human beings and, for example, I think it noble that no winter passed without* The Graphic *doing something to instill sympathy for the poor.*
>
> —The Hague, November 1, 1882

Increasingly, Goupil's prints of portraits of the wealthy, or of panoramic bygone battle scenes and exotic places, became irrelevant to Vincent in the scheme of contemporary life as he witnessed it. Gradually, Vincent became disillusioned with selling art devoid of any worthwhile purpose. Years later, after leaving his apprenticeship and becoming an artist himself, Vincent wrote to Theo, *I tell you that of all I have learned and heard at Goupil & Cie. about art, nothing has proven to be true* (Nuenen, on or about June 9, 1885).

RELIGION AS A REFUGE

> *It would not be easy to live without faith in Him and the old assurance in Him; without it, one would lose one's courage.*
>
> —Laken, on or about November 13, 15, or 16, 1878

After several years of training in The Hague, Vincent was sent to London where he worked at the Goupil branch for over a year. Initially he spent some very happy times there, exploring the city, taking long walks, working hard, and earning a good salary. He boarded at the home of a widow and her daughter and enjoyed the familial company. Things changed when he fell in love with the young woman but found out that she was already secretly engaged. He tried to persuade her to change her mind but to no avail. Her rejection hurt him deeply.

During a subsequent visit to Holland in the summer of 1874, his family noticed a significant change in his demeanor; his earlier optimism and enthusiasm was replaced by a downcast mood and lackluster attitude. His employers sent him to their branch in Paris for a few months hoping that a change of scenery would revive his spirits, as well as his ambition. It did but only insofar as he discovered there the artist Eugene Delacroix, whose treatise on art and on color he read with interest. Returning to London, he hadn't recovered his good spirits. Still feeling melancholy and dejected, he became more reclusive. He avoided social contacts, preferring to spend time in solitary musings or reading, or in creating scrapbooks for Theo with his favorite poems. Coupled with Vincent's dissatisfaction with the art he was selling and the rejection he had suffered, was a deeply nagging homesickness.

Vincent was also acutely aware how much he was encumbered by his lack of social refinement. His intensity and single-mindedness made it difficult for anyone to join him. This inability to connect with people was likened in his mind to the experience of rejection. The actual rejection by the daughter of his London landlord had opened a deep wound, one he carried within him since his youth.

As Vincent spiraled deeper into depression and unhappiness, he began to find his only anchor of comfort in the stories of the Bible. For the next few years he would fill his waking hours with passionate study of the Bible and other religious books. By May 1875, he was back again working in the Paris branch of Goupil for a ten-month stay, living in a cramped room in Montmartre. While he visited galleries and museums and found some consolation in seeing the art of Camille Corot and Jean-Francois Millet, he spent most of his time sequestered in his frugally furnished room reading the Bible, writing letters, and discussing religion with his roommate, a young man equally filled with religious fervor:

> *I cannot tell you how much I sometimes long for the Bible, I read something out of it daily, but I would so much like to know it by heart and look at life in the light of that word of which it is said: "Thy word is a lamp unto my feet, and a light unto my path."*
>
> —Dordrecht, March 16, 1877

On Sundays he attended church services, sometimes three times on a single day. Hearing and reading the Gospel stories, where he could identify with the suffering of Jesus, gave him the sense that there might be, after all, a meaning and purpose to his anguish. He read *The Life of Jesus* by Ernest Renan, who depicted Jesus as an incomparable man, who was yet approachable, real, and very human. Renan wrote in a style that was metaphorically evocative, and his visual imagery and descriptions of the agrarian parables rang true with Vincent's own experiences. Vincent was taken by the stories about the historical Jesus: the rabbi who walked through the fields of Galilee healing and alleviating the suffering he encountered, bringing good news to the poor, binding up the brokenhearted, comforting those who mourned, setting captives free. Jesus became the role model for Vincent. Just before coming to Paris, feeling very much uprooted and homeless, much like a missionary wandering the globe, he had sent a paraphrased quote from Renan as an appendix to a letter to Theo:

> *To act in the world one must die to oneself. The people that makes itself the missionary of a religious thought has no other country than that thought. Man is not on this earth merely to be happy; nor is he placed here merely to be simply honest, he is here to accomplish great things through society, to arrive at nobility, and to overcome the vulgarity that enslaves the existence of almost everyone.*
>
> —London, May 8, 1875

Vincent also read *The Imitation of Christ,* the devotional classic by Thomas à Kempis, a fifteenth-century priest and mystic who had lived in present-day Holland. À Kempis wrote this handbook to provide instructions for leading a spiritual life, with an emphasis on obedience to God and withdrawal from the world. Vincent hoped that by following such a path he would find validation for his own difficulties and gain a life of serenity and purpose. John Bunyan's *A Pilgrim's Progress* was another book that deeply preoccupied him, identifying with the quest of the main character, Christian, a man tormented by spiritual anguish. Christian is urged by a spiritual guide to enter upon a pilgrimage to reach the Celestial City where he will achieve salvation. Influenced by this story, Vincent too felt himself to be a pilgrim, ever searching for deliverance from his suffering.

In the last few months of his apprenticeship, Vincent filled page upon page of his letters with biblical quotes, hymns, extracts from the books he read, and summaries of sermons he had heard. At times his own voice was almost drowned out amid the deluge of excerpts from the myriad inspirational sources he was reading. While Vincent hoped such encouraging and inspirational letters would encourage Theo, who was also experiencing a barren time, the letters fulfilled his own needs too. *"For those who love God all things work together for good, is a beautiful saying. So it will be with you, and the aftertaste of these difficult days will be good"* (Paris, December 10, 1875).

A STRANGER ON THE EARTH

> *If you want to persevere and make spiritual progress, look upon yourself as an exile and a pilgrim on this earth.*
>
> —Thomas à Kempis

Vincent decided to visit his parents for Christmas, even though he was slated to work at the galleries throughout the holidays.

This unwarranted vacation, in addition to his lack of zeal in selling the artwork, prompted the Goupil establishment to give him notice, his dismissal effective in three months. During these last months in Paris, as he wrestled with the great shame of his failure, he began reading the novels of George Eliot, particularly *Felix Holt, the Radical,* and *Scenes of a Clerical Life.* These narratives deal with the struggles of hardworking decent people who sacrifice themselves for the good of others. Eliot's characters inspired Vincent and prompted a desire to imitate their actions. Such novels joined the many art prints he hung in his room, as companions on his pilgrim's path.

With the return to his parents' home in March 1876, Vincent broke forever with his career as an art dealer. He was unclear about what he wanted or should do next, although he felt that his future would somehow involve an effort to follow Jesus through preaching the Gospel, and he spent the ensuing five years of trials and failures trying to discover his purpose. Initially, thanks to his extensive religious reading, he secured a position teaching the catechism at a parochial boys' school in Ramsgate, England. While there Vincent returned to the thought he had first formulated in London, namely of becoming a missionary or a pastor among working-class people. George Eliot's novel *Silas Marner,* the story of a weaver sharing the hardships of the common laborer, reinforced this resolve. Vincent began to think seriously about following in his father's footsteps and becoming a clergyman. *Should I find anything, then it will probably be a position between clergyman and missionary in the suburbs of London among working-class people* (Welwyn, June 17, 1876). Such thoughts quickened his spirit, making him feel as if he was seeing *a light in the distance so clearly; should that light disappears now and then, it is my own fault.* He continued to read George Eliot, moved by her stories of the poor and destitute, and living vicariously alongside her characters:

> *There's such a longing for religion among the people in those big cities. Many a worker in a factory or shop has had a strangely pure, pious youth. But city life often takes away "the early dew of morning," however the longing for "the old, old story" remains, for the bottom of one's heart stays the bottom of one's heart. In one of her books, Eliot describes the life of factory workers etc. who have joined together in a small community and hold religious services in a chapel in 'Lantern Yard', and she says it is "God's Kingdom upon earth," nothing more or less.*
>
> —Isleworth, November 25, 1876

Following Eliot's lead, he wove elements of her story "Janet's Repentance" from *Scenes of a Clerical Life* into his own life.

> *I found the last story, "Janet's Repentance," especially moving. It is about the life of a curate who lives among the inhabitants of the dirty streets of a town. His study looked out over gardens with cabbage stalks etc. and over the red roofs and smoking chimneys of poor houses. For his midday meal he usually received badly cooked mutton and watery potatoes. At about the age of 34 he died, he had been nursed during his long illness by a woman who had previously fallen into drinking but, through his words and her reliance on him, had improved herself and found peace for her soul.*
>
> —Paris, February 19, 1876

Being still too young to apply for missionary training, he accepted the offer of becoming a curate in a Methodist parish in Isleworth where he also taught Bible classes in a school for poor and neglected boys. Even though he only earned his room and board, most likely eating cooked mutton and watery potatoes quite often, he seemed happy there, recounting to Theo how in the school:

> *One hears the cheerful sound of the boys learning their lessons . . . from time to time one of them begins humming the melody of some hymn or other, and in me I feel something of the "old faith." What I should wish to be I am not yet, but with God's help, I'll succeed. . . . No longer does a day pass without speaking about God. . . . At present my talks about Him aren't much yet, but with God's help and blessing that shall become better. . . . I think the Lord has taken me as I am, with all my faults, but I am still hoping for a more profound acceptance.*
>
> —Isleworth, August 26, 1876

What pleased Vincent most was that parish work, such as visiting the sick, would help him *find by and by what I want* (Isleworth, October 7 and 8, 1876). As a curate of several small churches in the parish he was also "*sent to preach the Gospel to the poor*" (Luke 4:18; cf. Isaiah 61:1):

> *But whoever wants to preach the Gospel must have it in his own heart first. Oh! That I might find it, for it is only the word spoken in simplicity and from the abundance of the heart that can bring forth fruit.*
>
> —Isleworth, October 13, 1876

Vincent added that in the future he would be preaching the Gospel wherever he went and related the feeling he had when standing in the pulpit for the first time. *Theo, last Sunday your brother spoke for the first time in God's house, in the place where it is written "in this place I will give peace"* (quoted from Jeremiah 14:13; Isleworth, November 3, 1876). It felt as if he were *emerging from a dark cave underground, coming back to the friendly daylight.*

He chose as his title "I am a stranger on this Earth" inspired by Bunyan's *Pilgrim's Progress* and by Thomas à Kempis' notion that people who are on a spiritual quest must consider themselves exiles and pilgrims. He included the whole sermon written in English, which began with these words:

> *It is an old faith and it is a good faith that our life is a pilgrim's progress; that we are strangers in the earth, but that though this be so, yet we are not alone for our Father is with us. We are pilgrims—our life is a long walk, a journey from earth to heaven.*
>
> —Isleworth, November 3, 1876

Walking and journeying were literally and figuratively woven together during these months in England. Vincent had to walk for hours to reach the little churches where he preached, often starting out at four in the morning. His letters became richly descriptive of the hikes he took, very often alluding to scenes where a "light shone in the darkness": twilight and daybreak, lamplit windows, the lights of a village seen in the distance. Once when he was lost on one of his long walks, he *at last saw a light in a little house* . . . [and] . . . *there was a beautiful small wooden church with a friendly light at the end of that dark road* (Isleworth, November 25, 1876). These were images of hope and a clarity he yearned for on his own inner journey. He also described how pleasing it was to see church spires silhouetted against the sky, reminding him of his father's parish in Holland, where *the lights in the village and the steeple between the snow-covered poplar trees* beckoned him from far away. And then he added, overcome by homesickness, *but it is love that gives so much beauty and animation to it all* (Isleworth, August 26, 1876).

Though as yet only with words, Vincent was already a passionate painter. In a little over ten years, he would be describing and animating such scenes with a brush. But now, the "light" of his true vocation was still far off in the distance. The undercurrent and latent desire to express himself more forcibly, more visibly, often left him restless, a "stranger on the earth," seeking but not yet finding. Yet many of the sights and the feelings, which he shared so copiously with Theo during this time, fed his soul and enriched his memories, sources that would eventually inspire his great works of art.

Besides sharing the descriptions of all that he saw with Theo, Vincent was also responding to the content of his brother's letters. Theo, who had begun his career as an art apprentice in The Hague, wrote about his own sense of loneliness, abandonment, and unhappiness in a strange city. Vincent could well identify with such feelings and offer consolation, filling his letters with Bible quotes and poems.

> *There are hours and days and times in life when God hides His face, as it were, but for those who love God even those times, those sad times, are not entirely without God, but as though full of prophecies for the future and full of voices from the past.*
>
> —Isleworth, between September 2 and 8, 1876

Vincent continued to urge his brother to *above all have love amongst each other so that God may strengthen and increase it.* And if sometimes there weren't people he could love enough, Theo should then love the town where he lived by seeking *to please the poor and to find favor in their eyes,* for didn't he, Vincent, also love Paris and London even though he was a child of the pine woods? He continued, *and let Christ be the center of your longing* (Isleworth, between September 2 and 8, 1876). As for himself, Vincent wrote, *I will seek the Love of Christ and strive to work for Him all my life.* To make Theo realize that he understood his anxiety and homesickness, Vincent recounted the time when he was left at the boarding school, watching the carriage of his parents disappear in the distance. A fortnight later when his father came unexpectedly to visit him, he fell around his neck. At that very moment, Vincent felt an immense closeness with his father, the closeness of a welcoming embrace that Vincent remembered from the print of the Prodigal Son hanging in his father's study. The meaning of the parable's message was brought into Vincent's experience:

> [It was] *a moment in which we both felt that we have a Father in heaven; because also my father looked up and in his heart there was an even bigger voice than mine crying "Abba, Father."*
>
> —Isleworth, between September 2 and 8, 1876

Vincent added that between that moment of experiencing the reality of the unconditional love of a Heavenly Father through his father's embrace *and today are years of pilgrimage,* years of exile and loneliness. *There is a saying that accompanies us and grows up with us, as it were, which is, "sorrowful, yet always rejoicing"* (2 Corinthians 6:10). Vincent wanted Theo to realize that despite the hardships now, he always had reason to rejoice because an unconditional love was at all times present to welcome him home. In this very long letter Vincent included all the scriptures he could think of that would encourage Theo, just as they supported and strengthened him.

> *The Lord is thy keeper. He is thy shade on thy right hand. In him is deliverance from death, in Him is everlasting life. My boy, there will come days when we shall no longer believe because we heard it said, but when we shall know and feel and love it. Then we shall be moved, when we hear the name of God pronounced, even as we are moved when we see our father again after having been gone from home for a long time.*
>
> —Isleworth, between September 2 and 8, 1876

ON THE ROAD AGAIN

> *Our nature is sorrowful, but for those who have learnt and are learning to look at Jesus Christ, there is always reason to rejoice. It is a good word that of St. Paul; as*

> *being sorrowful yet always rejoicing. For those who believe in Jesus Christ there is no death or sorrow that is not mixed with hope—no despair—there is only a constantly being born again, a constantly going from darkness into light.*
>
> —From Vincent's first sermon
> Isleworth, November 3, 1876

Despite the fulfillment he felt in preaching the Gospel in small churches around London, Vincent still suffered from being *away from home for a long time.* He was still in a place of doubt, still only seeing the *light at the end of that dark road,* still on that journey where there was *a constantly being born again, a constantly going from darkness into light* (Isleworth, November 3, 1876). In Isleworth there was no prospect of advancing toward greater responsibility or of making a living. After six months of dedication and engagement in parish work and in teaching and caring for the boys in the school, he returned to Holland. There, with no other plans yet in sight, he was hired as a clerk in a bookstore in the town of Dordrecht. But those who observed him at work affirmed what he felt, too—that he was unfit for the book-selling business.

Vincent sank into another bout of anxiety and depression and felt tired of everything, especially of running into dead ends. He wondered in a letter to Theo if this was a feeling to be avoided, or whether it was something one should not fear but cherish to *see if it may bring some good? Is it the "sorrowing for God" which leads us to make a choice which we never regret?* Vincent comforted himself by adding that at such times one should think of the following scripture passage, "*Come unto me, all ye that labor . . . and I will give you rest* (Matthew 11:28-30). "Still too young to enroll in missionary training, yet yearning to *be shown the way to devote my life more fully to the service of God and the Gospel*, Vincent began to formulate a new plan, that of going to Amsterdam to study theology:

> *Oh Theo, if it only could happen that the heavy depression that overpowers me, because of everything that I have tried has failed and because of the torrent of reproaches which I have heard and felt, might be taken from me and I could be given the necessary opportunity and the strength and love to develop fully and to persevere and remain standing in that for which my father and I would thank the Lord so fervently.*
>
> —Dordrecht, March 8, 1877

Vincent sorted through these desires and thoughts in long letters to Theo, seeking, as always, to give them a more tangible shape. Believing that he could succeed in the thing he so earnestly desired, which was at present to follow in his father's footsteps, Vincent wrote with renewed optimism:

> *Just as for a "sower of God's word," which I hope to be, and for a sower of the seed in the fields, each day will bring enough of its own evil, and the earth will produce many thorns and thistles. Let us continue to support each other and seek brotherly love.*
>
> —Dordrecht, April 22 and 23, 1877

Meanwhile at the bookstore, instead of the job he had been hired to do, he often hid in the back room hard at a self-appointed task: to translate the Bible from Dutch into German. On Sundays he continued to attend worship services, often visiting denominations other than the Dutch Reformed Church. Questioned about this habit by one of his fellow boarders, he replied, "Do you really think that God cannot be found in the other churches?" Even though his employers considered Vincent a gentle and pleasant fellow, he wasn't selling many books, and they dismissed him after only three months. By that time, Vincent had solidified his plan to begin theological studies and had rallied his family's support. Feeling encouraged, Vincent continued to read and study.

> [I managed] *to work my way through the whole story of Christ from a catechism book . . . and I copied out the texts, which reminded me of so many paintings by Rembrandt and others. It is, I believe and trust, a choice not to be repented of* [of becoming a Christian laborer]. *Yes, all the things of the past can work together for good, for through the experience with cities like London and Paris and life in such places as that school in Ramsgate and in Isleworth, one is more drawn and attached to many things and to the books of the Bible.*
>
> —Dordrecht, April 30, 1877

Taking further stock of what he had learned, and indicating his developing conviction that art and religion were strongly entwined, he added,

> *Familiarity with and love for the work and life of such men as Jules Breton, Millet and Jacque, Rembrandt, Bosboom, and so many others, can also become a source to get ideas.*
>
> —Dordrecht, April 30, 1877

Vincent moved to Amsterdam in May 1877. True to his tradition of visual learning and *to give it the right atmosphere for new thoughts and ideas* (Amsterdam, May 19, 1877), Vincent covered the walls of his room with biblical images. Embarking on this new venture, Vincent could identify very strongly with Theo's ongoing efforts to come to terms with the demands of his apprenticeship. Theo, in his discouragement, had written that he wished he were *far away from everything; . . . I alone have brought all this sadness on myself and others* (Amsterdam, May 30, 1877). In his response, Vincent included a quote from the New Testament about Jesus sending the discouraged fishermen, his disciples, back out again to try once more to catch fish.

And then he continued, letting his brother know that his words had struck a chord, *because that same feeling, exactly the same, neither more nor less, is also on my conscience* (Amsterdam, May 30, 1877):

> *When we are working at a difficult task and strive after something good, then we fight the good fight of which the direct reward is that we are spared from much evil. And God sees the trouble and sorrow, and He can help in spite of everything. Faith in God is strong in me—it is not imagination, nor idle faith. It is so. It is true—there is a God Who is alive—and he is with our parents, and His eye is also upon us; and I am sure that he has His purpose for our life and that we, as it were, do not quite belong to ourselves—and this God is no other than Christ about Whom we read in our Bible and Whose word and history is also deep in your heart—had I but sooner given all my strength to it before, yes, then things would have been better for me now—but even now He will be a mighty help and it is in His power to make our lives bearable, to keep us from evil, to let all things work together for good, to make our end peaceful.*
>
> —Amsterdam, May 30, 1877

Once again, in his encouraging words to Theo, Vincent was also writing to himself, remembering that, despite the difficulties of life, there were also those happy moments when heart and soul rejoiced, like hearing a lark singing in the morning. They had to continue to be mindful of such moments and store them within their memories; Vincent had done this since childhood. The recollection of everything they had ever loved would always succeed in uplifting them. More than ever Vincent needed to hear his own advice, for he was oppressed by the preparatory study and the entrance exams that loomed ever larger before him. Yet he was still motivated to reach his aim:

> [becoming] *a good minister, who has something to say that is good and useful in the world, and perhaps it is good after all that I have a relatively long time of preparation and become secure in a firm conviction before I'm called upon to speak about it to others. It is right that before one begins such work, one should gather together a wealth of things that could benefit others.*
>
> —Amsterdam, April 3, 1878

He had to hire a tutor to help him with his biggest stumbling block, the study of Latin and Greek, which in his opinion was not the *wealth of things that could benefit others*. His tutor Mendes da Costa recalled Vincent exclaiming to him in utter frustration, "Mendes, do you seriously believe that such horrors are indispensable to a man who wants to do what I want to do: give peace to poor creatures and reconcile them to their existence here on earth?" While in England he had already determined the constituents of his future ministry: the people who lived in darkness—the weavers, and especially, the miners. Vincent added: "John Bunyan's Pilgrim's Progress is of much more use to me, and Thomas à Kempis and a translation of the Bible, and I don't want anything more." The weeks in Amsterdam spent in tortuous study of subjects he didn't believe would benefit anyone were leading Vincent downward toward another failed attempt on his journey.

Vincent resorted increasingly to the one occupation that kept him going: the act of writing, which allowed him to "think visually." By using Theo as his sounding board he could more clearly define his innermost frame of mind, his questions, and his uncertainties. Both brothers had been engaged for some time in discussing their duties and their vocations. Both Theo, on his way to becoming an art dealer, and Vincent, aiming to be an evangelist, were preparing for work that gave them a sense of self-worth as well as acceptance from their father. Yet, Vincent feared that he once again would not live up to his family's expectations.

Letters from Amsterdam overflowed with his favorite scripture passages, often making no distinction when his words ended and scripture began. Writing these long soul-searching epistles was cathartic. He could lighten his burden by sharing it with Theo. Gradually he was working through his decision to give up academic studies, though not his quest to become an honest and spiritual man. To this he was still duty-bound:

> *It is good to be an "honnête homme"* [an honest man] *and try to be that more and indeed almost and altogether and it is good if one believes that being an "homme intérieur et spirituel"* [a spiritual man with an inner life] *is part of it. If one only knew for certain that one belonged among them, one would always go one's way, calmly and collectedly, never doubting that things would turn out well in the end. . . .*
>
> *As far as being an "homme intérieur et spirituel," couldn't one develop that in oneself through knowledge of history in general and of certain people of all times, in particular from biblical times to the Revolution and from* The Odyssey *to the books of Dickens and Michelet? And couldn't one learn something from the work of the likes of Rembrandt.*
>
> *The ray from on high doesn't always shine on us, and is sometimes behind clouds, and without that light a human being cannot live and has no worth and can do nothing good, and anyone who claims that one can live without faith in that higher light and doesn't worry about attaining it will end up being deceived. We've talked quite a lot about what we feel to be our duty and how we should arrive at something good, and we rightly came to the conclusion that first of all our goal must be to find a certain position and a profession to which we can devote ourselves completely. . . .*

> *As far as I'm concerned, I must become a good minister, who has something to say that is good and that can be useful in the world.*
>
> —Amsterdam, April 3, 1878

Reading the Gospel and the Epistles of John about the love of God, Vincent was reminded again and again that love would overcome all. God loved humanity, and human beings were to love one another. This was the force that would keep him going despite another failure:

> *It is good to have as much love as one can, for therein lies true strength, and he who loves much can do much and is capable of much, and that which is done with love is well done.*
>
> *Love is the best and most noble thing in the human heart, especially when it has been tried and tested in life like gold in the fire, happy is he and confident in himself who has loved much and, even if he has wavered and doubted, has kept that divine fire and has returned to that which was there in the beginning and shall never die. If one but continues to love faithfully that which is truly worthy of love, and does not waste one's love on truly trivial and insignificant and faint-hearted things, then one gradually will get more and more light and become stronger.*
>
> *The sooner one seeks to become competent in a certain position and in a certain profession, and acquires a fairly independent way of thinking and acting, and the more one observes fixed rules, the stronger one's character becomes, but that does not mean that one has to become narrow-minded. . . . If one is competent in one thing and understands one thing well, one gains at the same time insight into and knowledge of many other things. . . .*

> *One should never trust it when one is without difficulties or without some worry or obstacle, and not make things too easy for oneself. Even in the most civilized circles and the best environment and circumstances, one should retain something of the original nature of a Robinson Crusoe or of an uncultured human being, for otherwise one has no root in oneself, and one should never let the fire in one's soul go out but keep it going, for there will always be an opportunity where this will be useful.*
>
> —Amsterdam, April 3, 1878

Within this long letter, Vincent justified his decision to abandon his course of study while reassuring Theo that he would carry on. He still had his faith! Despite another dead-end, *the fire in his soul*—his desire to bring the light of the Gospel to the poor—remained. Deep down, he knew that he had to keep striving for something to which he could devote himself in body, mind, and spirit, and it wasn't the study of ancient languages or years of academic work:

> *Happy is he who has faith in God, for he shall, although not without struggle and sorrow and life's difficulties, overcome in the end. One cannot do better than, amidst everything in all circumstances, in all places and at all times, to hold fast to the thought of God and to strive to learn more of Him; one can do this through the Bible, as well as through all other things.*
>
> *It is good to go on believing that everything is full of wonder, more so than one can comprehend, for that is the truth; it is good to remain sensitive and lowly and meek in heart, even though one has to hide that feeling sometimes, because that is often necessary; it is good to be very learned about the things that are hidden from the wise and the educated of the world but are*

> *revealed instinctively to the poor and simple, to women and babes.*
>
> *For what can one learn that is better than what God has put by nature into every human soul, namely that which in the depths of every soul lives and loves, hopes and believes, unless it is wantonly destroyed?*
>
> *So let us just go on quietly, each on his own path, always following the light "sursum corda"*["Let us raise our hearts on high"].
>
> —Amsterdam, April 3, 1878

After more than a year in a fruitless pursuit of a university degree, Vincent took stock of all that had given him meaning throughout the years: the poor, the natural world, stories, pictures, the desire to be useful and to perform his duty. This enabled him to continue on in his own path, refocussing his sight on the distant light, and the light he hoped to share with the people walking in darkness:

> *Living and loving, hoping and believing, in the depth of every soul. . . . This is the creed which all good men have expressed in their works, all who have thought more deeply and looked for more and worked more and loved more than others, they are the ones that have dived into the depths of the sea of life. We too must cast ourselves into the depths if we want to catch something, and if sometimes it happens that we have to toil all night and catch nothing, then it is good not to give up yet but in the morning cast out the net again. . . . We are today what we were yesterday, namely "honest men," men who must be tried in the fire of life to become strengthened and steadfast within, and become, through the Grace of God, what we are by nature.*
>
> —Amsterdam, April 3, 1878

3

Light in the Darkness

You surely know that one of the roots or fundamental truths, not only of the Gospel but of the entire Bible, is "the light that dawns in the darkness." "Through darkness to light." Well then, who will most certainly need it, who will have ears to hear it?

Experience has taught that those who work in darkness, in the heart of the earth like the miners in the black coal mines, among others, are very moved by the message of the Gospel and also believe it.

—Laken, on or about November 13 and 15, or 16, 1878

MISSIONARY-IN-TRAINING

If I could spend three years or so in a similar region, working in peace and continuously learning and observing, then I wouldn't come back from there without having something to say that is indeed worth hearing; with all humility, yet with frankness I say this. There are in the Borinage already several small Protestant congregations. . . . I wish I could get a position there as an evangelist just as we talked about it, preaching the Gospel to the poor—those who need it most and for whom it is so well meant . . . and then applying myself to teaching during the week.

—Laken, on or about November 13 and 15, or 16, 1878

Having reached the proper age of twenty-five, Vincent applied to the Training School for Evangelist Missionaries in Brussels, which offered a much shorter course of study. What was demanded by the school was less knowledge of dead languages and theology, but a greater aptitude for practical work. Applicants had to have a strong faith and oratory skills. Vincent was accepted. While at the school and taking walks through the town, he learned about a mining district in Belgium called the Borinage. The miners came into town with their loads of coal and Vincent encountered them in a local pub. There he could observe and interact with them; he even included a little sketch of this pub in a letter to Theo, something he had done from time to time to commemorate certain places. He had come to believe that these men, covered in black soot, were truly a people who lived in darkness.

After three months training at the missionary school, Vincent was not given an assignment, despite his zeal. Even though the missionary training was not as rigorous as the preparatory studies for the university, he had never functioned well in an academic setting. He was an obstinate student who had trouble adhering to rules that he felt to be worthless. As he was not Flemish, he was also told that he would need greater financial resources in order to remain at the school. Vincent left with the conviction that he would gain a better education in a *free course at the great university of misery* (Cuesmes, between June 22 and 24, 1880) where he would learn the experiential way. The lack of authorization from the missionary school would not stanch his resolve to seek out the poorest possible missionary field, in the mining district of the Borinage:

> *You see, it always strikes me and it is something remarkable, when we see the image of unspeakable and indescribable abandonment—of loneliness—of poverty and misery, the extreme end of things—the thought of God arises in our mind. At least this is the case with me.*
>
> —Laken, on or about November 13 and 15, or 16, 1878

MISSIONARY TO THE MINERS

Now, there is in the south of Belgium, in Hainaut, from around the area of Mons to the French borders and even extending far beyond, a region called the Borinage, where there is a peculiar population of laborers who work in the numerous coal mines. I found this amongst other things about them in a geography booklet: The Borins (the inhabitants of the Borinage) do nothing but mine coal.

—Laken, on or about November 13 and 15, or 16, 1878

With unshakable determination to be a sower of God's word and with the address of a local pastor in hand, Vincent arrived in Pâturages, a small mining town in the Borinage in December 1878. Here he would begin his career as an evangelist of the Gospel. With his proper Dutch manners and a good knowledge of French he made a favorable impression and was given the task to teach Sunday School and visit the sick. He received room and board from the vendor, Van der Haegen, in exchange for tutoring his children in the evenings. His new tasks amid the poor laborers became for Vincent a conscious and practical experiment in discipleship. He was on the path that would lead him toward fulfilling what "set his soul on fire"—ministering to the poor, as Jesus had done.

Though the example of Jesus' ministry was almost two thousand years old, for Vincent it was a call to follow in the here and now in a nineteenth-century mining town. Jesus had taught a way of life by living that life; he had formed relationships with the men and women in the places he passed through and embraced them regardless of who they were or what they did. Jesus saw people's needs and responded with compassion. The misery and poverty Vincent witnessed called him to take action in a similar manner. Vincent intended to become fully present to the poor in this most desolate mission field where, he felt, Jesus would have been found shining his Father's light into the miners' darkness, healing the sick, and bringing hope to the hopeless. When members of the missionary society decided to check on their renegade pupil, they noted his efforts and devotion, and in January 1879 granted Vincent a probationary nomination for six months as missionary in the Borinage.

He was given the assignment of preaching to a small congregation in the town of Wasmes, in the room of a building called Salon du Bébé. It was a tight space but a place where Vincent could put all his knowledge of scriptures and religious readings into passionate Gospel messages. A small crowd of miners and their families attended his services in the cramped room, taking a short respite from the daily drudge of a life governed by the mine. For these men and women hardly anything else existed but the continuous rhythms of being lowered into and hoisted out of the bowels of the earth. Vincent wrote extensively about his life among the miners and learned that one had to understand the miners' temperament and nature and approach them without *pretensions, pride or a sense of superiority, otherwise one can't get on with them and could never win their trust* (Wasmes, between April 1 and 16, 1879). These men and many women, children and youth, spent more than half of each day down in the mines. They barely saw sunlight. Those who lived above the ground during daylight hours, mostly wives and mothers, toiled in small cottages, tending to meager soot-covered gardens, and battling the constant invasion of coal dust into their sparsely furnished homes. They lived among trees deadened and black from smoke, walked along paths where only thorn hedges could thrive, past dunghills, ash dumps, and heaps of useless coal. It was a desolate and hostile environment. Sanitary conditions in the mines were abysmal, and everyone suffered from multiple diseases and had no access to adequate health care. Furthermore, there was the constant threat of mine explosions and accidents. And yet these miners toiled ceaselessly to supply the coal that warmed city homes and fueled new industrial factories. How was Vincent to make the love and light of the Gospel relevant to those who were leading such sacrificial lives in abject poverty and darkness? When he looked into the soot-stained and emaciated faces of the motley group of parishioners before his makeshift pulpit, he realized that mere words wouldn't reach into the core of their misery to bring light into their gloomy hopelessness.

Vincent began to move beyond the confinements and rules of religious institutions and sought more practicable ways to integrate Jesus' message into his missionary work. He set about the task of getting to know and befriend the miners and their families. Beholding their predicament firsthand confirmed his conviction that not by preaching, but by doing *unto others as you would have them to do unto you* (Matthew 7:12) would he make a difference in their lives. This, he believed, was the way to live that made the holy mystery of the Gospel a reality. He visited them in their homes and gave them some relief by helping with their daily chores. Seeing a sick miner unable to get up from his pallet of straw he sat down on the floor beside him, talking and praying with the man. Sometimes he nursed the injured back to health, ripping his own bed linens or his only shirt into bandages. When one of the miners was so badly injured in a mining explosion that he was given up for lost, Vincent devoted his time to nursing him back to life. In order to better understand and experience the same hardships, he made the decision to live as the poorest among them, denying himself all comfort. He moved out of his host's home and found a hovel where he slept on the ground. He wanted to live in true solidarity with those who were suffering the most so he would better know how to serve them. When his hostess protested he said to her, "Esther, one should do like the good God; from time to time one should go and live among His own."

It is said that he was often heard weeping at night alone in his hut—from the cold, from hunger, and from being overcome by the endless efforts needed to bring relief and restore hope. Thomas à Kempis' call to renounce all worldly ambition and embrace poverty had inspired Vincent. He felt that only by entering into the miners' experience of desperation, deprivation, vulnerability, and hopelessness would he be following the example of Jesus "living among His own." Vincent even descended into the mineshaft, which he called *the pit of hell*, in order to see the miners' world first hand. When a miners' strike broke out Vincent stood up to the mining bosses and advocated for miners' rights at a time when the poor had no rights at all. Such devotion was unheard of by missionaries who had been sent into the field to preach. Vincent had taken the example of Jesus as the guideline for his deeds.

In the course of the six months of the probationary period granted by the missionary society, Vincent had forsaken all personal comfort in order to live as close to a miner's life as possible. He had committed himself so entirely to this solidarity that he had begun to look like a miner himself. He had become emaciated, ill, and dressed in tattered rags. When the missionary society sent their emissary to check on him, Vincent was barely recognizable. The society did not approve of his efforts to follow Jesus' teachings so literally. Believing that Vincent was an embarrassment, they withdrew their support in July 1879. According to the official documents, Vincent van Gogh was dismissed due to a lack of oratory skills necessary for preaching. Vincent knew otherwise and voiced his opinion a year later:

> *I must tell you that with evangelists it is the same as with artists. There is an old academic school, often hateful and tyrannical, abominably desolate, in fact—men who like in an armor, wear a steel cuirass of prejudices and conventions. When these people are in charge of affairs, they dispose of positions, and by a system of circumlo-*

cution seek to maintain their protégés in their places at the exclusion of the ordinary man. Their God is like the God of the drunkard Falstaff in Shakespeare. Some of these evangelical gentlemen find themselves by a strange coincidence (perhaps if they were capable of human feeling, they themselves would be somewhat surprised) with the same point of view that that drunken character has on spiritual matters.

—Cuesmes, between June 22 and 24, 1880

Vincent was well aware that one of the reasons he was now unemployed, and once again a pilgrim on his road, was *that I have different ideas than the gentlemen who grant positions to men who think as they do* (Cuesmes, between June 22 and 24, 1880). Rejected by the religious establishment, he had brought another shame upon his family. His father could not agree with his son's desire to follow the teaching of Thomas à Kempis by "choosing a life of poverty" and had even threatened to commit Vincent to an insane asylum. In his opinion, Vincent had gone too far in his devotion to the mining classes and had now, after his dismissal, become lazy, aimless, and dysfunctional. To make matters worse, Theo too judged Vincent to be idle and irresponsible for failing to comply with both his family's as well as the missionary society's expectations. Theo felt his brother was deteriorating in all aspects of social and familial norm; he was doing nothing about it and going downhill. Vincent admitted that he had lost time in terms of earning a living and that the outcome of his attempted studies was dismal. But was this in fact due to "going down" or "doing nothing?" He knew he would be asked "But what is your aim?" All he could say was that he had to continue on the path he had chosen, and that the answers would come, and his goal would become:

more definite, and will stand out slowly and surely, as the rough draft becomes a sketch, and the sketch becomes a picture . . . by working seriously on it, by pondering over the idea.

—Cuesmes, between June 22 and 24, 1880

THE INNER SPARK—THE FIRE IN OUR SOUL

Do our inner thoughts show outwardly? Someone may have a great fire in his soul, yet no one ever comes to warm himself at it, and the passers-by see but a little smoke coming out the chimney, and continue on their way. Look here, now, what must be done, tend that inner fire, have salt in oneself, wait patiently yet with how much impatience? Wait for the hour, I say, until someone will come and sit down, to stay?

—Cuesmes, between June 22 and 24, 1880

Following his dismissal, Vincent remained in the Borinage and the days that followed were the most bitter of his life; he wandered about feeling ill, wrought with worries, without any prospects to make a living, forsaken by his family and the church. It was during this time that Theo announced to Vincent that he would come to see him, urged by their parents to intervene and find a way to bring his wayward brother to his senses. Vincent anticipated Theo's arrival with great relief. The two brothers went for a long walk and Vincent reveled in Theo's company, feeling their closeness and their affection for each other. Vincent did admit that he was desperately homesick and very lonely. He longed for the embrace and acceptance of his family:

When one lives with others and is bound by a feeling of affection, then one is conscious of a reason for being, that one might not be entirely worthless and superfluous but perhaps is good for one thing or another, considering that we need each other and are making the same journey as travelling companions.

> *As much as everyone else, I need dealings of friendship or affection or trusting companionship and am not like a street pump or lamp post, whether of stone or iron, so that I can't do without them without feeling, like any other most civilized and decent man, a void and a lack—and I tell you these things to let you know what a healing effect your visit had on me.*
>
> *And just as I wished that we would not drift apart, I also wish this with regard to those at home.*
>
> —Cuesmes, between August 11 and 14, 1879

Theo urged Vincent to leave the Borinage and find respectable work. Vincent noted that when he had tried to follow the advice of his family and made plans for improvement and change, the results had not been good. The time when he had hoped to receive his father's approval through the studies in Amsterdam had been a disaster. He much preferred the days of care and difficulty in the Borinage. He felt he had learned more from life experiences than anything that was taught at an academy and announced to Theo that he would remain in the Borinage. The brothers' relationship became strained. Following Theo's visit, Vincent didn't write to his brother for eight and a half months.

No longer a missionary on probation, Vincent left the shack he had been staying in and moved to Cuesmes, another town in the Borinage. There he boarded with the miner Charles Decrucq, who let him share his children's bedroom. This miner was particularly attached to Vincent because of the way he had nursed his little son back to health following a desperate bout with typhoid fever.

Alone, without any ties to the outside world, Vincent continued to shed the familial, religious, and social constraints. Family connections that could have led to respectable positions were severed. He eschewed his brother's encouraging support. He had received no approval from religious institutions for his effort to ease the miners' lives, an effort that had taken a devastating toll on his personal health. He was weak and ill and without any support. But what he did have was his own humanity and his faith—his faith *in the ray from on high* (Amsterdam, April 3, 1878). With that little bit of light shining into his own pit of hell he maintained a glimmer of hope. In that cold dark place with nothing to distract him, he finally became aware of a light within his soul, a vital spark—the urge to create. He had always had a latent desire to make sketches and drawings, which he sometimes inserted in his letters. Just before entering the Borinage he had written to Theo that he would really like to

> *start making rough sketches of one or the other of the many things one meets along the way, but considering that it would actually not take me very far and that it would most likely keep me from my real work, it is better I don't begin.*
>
> —Laken, on or about November 13 and 15 or 16, 1878

At the time he wrote those words, immersed in coursework required by the missionary training school, he had suppressed his longing. But now, in the cramped bedroom of the miner's hut with nothing else he could do, he took up a pencil and began to *draw far into the night, to keep some souvenir and to strengthen the thoughts raised involuntarily by the aspect of things here* (Cuesmes, August 5, 1879).

During the next eight months, by the light of a flickering candle, while the miner's children were asleep, Vincent sketched. And slowly his spirits began to rise, rekindling at the same time the passion for all the art that had fed his soul in the past. He found courage and hope, affirmation and inspiration, in the rich store of his remembrances. He had once written to Theo how rich art was, and that if one could remember the things one had seen, one would never feel alone. For almost three years he had lived in a place devoid of art, except for the few prints Theo had sent him. But this long absence from the world of literature and art hadn't dimmed his appreciation and need for it. On the contrary, that world had remained embedded within his consciousness. Vincent's love for art had made his suffering bearable. The memory of artworks had helped him see in the darkened soot-covered world of the miners glimpses of scenes worthy of paintings. He had come to the Borinage with the ability to see with the eye of an artist. This country was unique, *everything speaks, as it were, and is full of character* (Wasmes, December 26, 1878). *Every moment there is something that moves one intensely* (Wasmes, between March 4 and 31, 1879). When he took his walks through the labyrinthine streets, lined with grimy brick houses on either side, or ventured beyond the towns where slag piles obscured the horizon, he was reminded of certain aspects and moods seen in great works of art:

> *There is a place nearby from where one can see in the distance below a large part of the Borinage, with the chimneys, mountains of coal, small workers' homes, the moving about of small black figures during the day just like in an ant heap, in the far distance dark fir woods with small white workers' cottages in front of them, a couple of little towers in the distance, an old mill etc. Usually a kind of fog hangs over it all, or there is the whimsical effect of light and dark because of the shadows caused by clouds that remind one of paintings by Rembrandt or Michel or Ruisdael.*
>
> —Wasmes, on or about June 19, 1879

The prints that he now hung on the walls of the miner's bedroom spurred him on. He returned to reading the books he had with him. And instead of writing letters to Theo, he relied on drawing to strengthen his thoughts and reconnect with all that had given him the greatest meaning.

Nevertheless, Theo had not forsaken Vincent. A small sum of money that he sent caused Vincent to break his long silence. Thanking Theo for his monetary support, Vincent wrote one of his most personal and moving letters, explaining to his brother what he had learned in his isolation, and how he had endured and survived:

> *When I was in different surroundings, surrounded by paintings and works of art, you well know that at that time I took a violent passion for those things that went as far as enthusiasm. And I don't regret it, but now, far from those surroundings again, I often feel homesick for the country of paintings.*
>
> *You may perhaps remember that I knew very well (and it may well be that I still know) what Rembrandt was or what Millet was, or Jules Dupré or Delacroix or Millais or M. Maris.*
>
> *Good—now I no longer have those surroundings—yet that something that's called soul, one claims that it never dies and that it lives forever and seeks forever and forever and for evermore.*
>
> *So instead of succumbing to homesickness, I said to myself, one's country or native land is everywhere. So instead of giving in to despair, I chose the path of active melancholy as long as I had the strength to function, or in other words, I preferred the melancholy that hopes and aspires and searches to the one that despairs, is mournful and stagnant.*
>
> —Cuesmes, between June 22 and 24, 1880

In this first letter after eight months, Vincent expressed himself with a new confident tone. He wrote in his own voice without relying on quotes or alluding to scripture. By now everything he had read had sunk deeply into his soul and through his life experiences had become transformed into beliefs that he could claim as his own. In the days of his deepest discouragement, when he took the way of active melancholy, the light of new hope and purpose had begun to dawn. This resumption of his correspondence with Theo—his lifeline—filled a tremendous void. All the thoughts and moments of life he had yearned to share with Theo poured forth onto the pages of this letter. He was emerging from his "pit of hell."

Vincent related the experience of a long journey by foot he had taken earlier, a walk out of the Borinage to the French town of Courrieres, with the hopes of encountering one of the artists he admired who lived there, Jules Breton. Upon arriving at Courrieres he found he didn't have the courage to knock on Breton's door and, having no money, walked all the way back to Cuesmes. It took him three days, sleeping in an abandoned carriage one night, in a woodpile and a haystack the other two nights. He saw many beautiful sights along the way, and wrote elaborate descriptions that could "paint" the scenery in Theo's mind. These three days in a beautiful countryside revitalized his mood. Though his mission to see Breton had not been fulfilled, the walk had given him a chance to think some more and to perceive a landscape free of coal dust and slag heaps. Seeing nature in brighter colors, blooming and verdant, helped lift the dark gloom that had weighed him down. When Vincent began to paint, he would become more aware that colors had a power of their own; they were a language unto themselves—the language of the soul, as the German philosopher Goethe had proclaimed. Vincent had read Goethe's poems and studied Delacroix's treatise on the powerful, often unconscious effect colors had on the human psyche. On this walk through the brighter and purer hues of nature, he experienced the effect they had on him: they animated his soul and brightened his sight enabling him to think with greater clarity, refresh his memories, and answer his own questions, such as *How can I be useful. Of what service can I be? There is something inside of me, what can it be?*

> *Well, and notwithstanding, it was in this extreme misery that I felt my vigor return and that I said to myself, "in*

any event I'll overcome it, I'll take up my pencil that I put down in my great discouragement and I'll get back into drawing," and from then on, it seems to me, everything has changed for me, and now I'm on my way and my pencil has become somewhat compliant and seems to become more so day by day. It was misery, too long and too severe, that had discouraged me to the point where I could no longer do anything.

I couldn't tell you how happy I feel to have resumed drawing again. It had already preoccupied me for a long time, but I always considered the thing impossible and beyond my reach. But now, while feeling both my weakness and my painful dependence in respect of many things, I've recovered my peace of mind, and my energy is returning day by day.

—Cuesmes, September 24, 1880

The self-knowledge and wisdom he had gained during the time in Cuesmes made him confidently respond to the accusation of his family that he had wasted his time with the miners, committing the sin of idleness. Finally Vincent could explain what he perceived to have transpired during the years of isolation in the Borinage and liberate himself from the burden of guilt for his failures. He discerned that what to his family was idleness following his work with the miners was rather a time of deep contemplation:

I should be very glad if somehow you could see in me something more than a sort of idle fellow, because there are two kinds of idleness that are in contrast to each other.

There is the man who is idle from laziness and from lack of character, by the baseness of his nature.

Then there is the idle man who is idle in spite of himself, who is inwardly consumed by a great longing for action but who does nothing, because it is impossible for him to do anything, because he seems to be imprisoned by something, because he does not possess what he needs to become productive, because the casualty of his circumstances bring him to that point. Such a man does not always know what he could do but feels instinctively, but I am good for something! I feel my life has a purpose! I know that I could be quite a different man! How can I be useful, of what service can I be? There is something inside of me, what is it? This is quite a different kind of idle man; if you like, you may judge me to be such a one!

—Cuesmes, between June 22 and 24, 1880

A NEW LANGUAGE

There is something of Michelet and of Delacroix in Victor Hugo, and there is something of Rembrandt in the Gospels or something of the Gospels in Rembrandt, whatever you like, it comes to more or less the same, provided that one understands it wisely, without trying to turn it in the wrong direction, . . . there is something of Rembrandt in Shakespeare.

—Cuesmes, between June 22 and 24, 1880

Rembrandt goes so deep into the mysterious that he says things for which there are no words in any language.

—Nuenen, on or about October 10, 1885

Vincent had the *something inside of* him all along. Throughout his childhood he was taught values and biblical truths through the narrative quality of images. He was visually literate and understood that art had an expressive power; it could console, comfort, enlighten, encourage and make abstract concepts concrete. He had instinctively employed this verbal-pictorial tradition in his letters home by sometimes including quick sketches with his written descriptions. And he had always been drawn to artists whose subject engaged him and affected him emotionally. Artists like Rembrandt, Millet, and Delacroix had created visual parables that communicated effectively. These were artists whose art was not solely done for the sake of creating an aesthetically pleasing and decorative picture, but who intended to express something of life that could fill the viewer with emotion, recognition, and understanding. Vincent tried to make Theo understand that his so-called idleness had been a time of deep transformation, a time to discover that all his learning and observing, his need *continually to educate myself, to study, if you like, precisely as I need to eat my bread,* had a purpose (Cuesmes, between June 22 and 24, 1880).

> *Someone, to give an example, will love Rembrandt, seriously, that man will know there is a God, he'll believe firmly in Him.*
>
> *Someone will make a deep study of the history of the French Revolution—and he will not be an unbeliever, he will see that in great events, too, there is a higher power that manifests itself.*
>
> *Someone will have attended, for a short time only, a free course at the great university of misery, and will have paid attention to the things he sees with his eyes and hears with his ears, and will have reflected about it; he too, will finish by believing, and will perhaps learn more about it than he could say.*
>
> *Try to understand the last word of what the great artists, the serious masters, say in their masterpieces: God will be found there. Someone has written or said it in a book, someone in a painting.*
>
> *And quite simply read the Bible, and the Gospels, because that will give you something to think about,*

> *and a great deal to think about and everything to think about, well then, think about this "great deal," think about "this everything," it raises your thinking above the ordinary, despite yourself. Since we know how to read, well then let's read!*
>
> —Cuesmes, between June 22 and 24, 1880

The time of so-called idleness had led him to recognize his soul's desire to create an art where *there will be God in it.* Art could point to a greater revelation, to glimpses of recognition of a "Something on High." Art quickened the spirit—Vincent had experienced this quickening many times while standing before a painting.

Art was the language that could say things for which there were no spoken words. Art could be his language. Like Rembrandt, he too could point to the mysterious, the sacred inherent in life. That is what Vincent wanted to explore: the deeper and larger aspects of life through the creation of art. Art would be the path upon which he could continue learning and striving to become "l'homme interieure et spirituel."

Reading more, observing more and learning all he could about creating an art language became Vincent's new religious vocation. He now unreservedly gave in to his urge to draw.

A NEW CREED

> *But you see, there are many things that one must believe and love. . . . The best way of knowing God is to love many things.*
>
> —Cuesmes, between June 22 and 24, 1880

During their walk together in the Borinage, Theo had told Vincent that he didn't recognize his brother anymore, he had changed so much. Vincent now responded:

> *On your last visit this past summer, when we walked together near the disused mine they call La Sorcière, you*

reminded me that there was a time when we also walked together near the old canal and mill of Rijswijk, and then, you said, we were in agreement on many things, but, you added—since then you've really changed, you are not the same any more.

Well, that's not quite how it is; what has changed is that then my life was less difficult and my future seemed less dark, but as to my inner self, as far as my way of seeing and thinking are concerned, they have not changed. However, if in fact there were a change, it is that now I think and I believe, and I love more seriously what I already thought, believed and loved then.

Therefore you mustn't think that I'm rejecting this or that; I am kind of a believer in my unbelief, and though having changed I am the same, and my torment is none other than this: what could I be good for, could I not serve and be useful in some way, how could I come to know more, and go more deeply into this subject or that?
—Cuesmes, between June 22 and 24, 1880

All the suffering Vincent had witnessed and endured had brought him to a new depth of his humanity. In the dark lonely place of his abandonment, he had experienced the transformative power of a Divine Grace. When he had nothing to fall back on, he found his innermost sense of being: *that something that's called soul* that *never dies* and *lives forever and seeks forever* (Cuesmes, between June 22 and 24, 1880). In a sense Vincent experienced a new birth. From his three years in the desolate wilderness of the Borinage, where he had been, despite it all, *always learning and observing,* he came forth with *something to say that was really worth hearing* and eventually worth seeing (Laken, on or about November 13 and 15, or 16, 1878). He had a clearer purpose in life that was defined by who he was at his core. He had come closer to his own truth and did not feel the need to live the truths of others, including his father. He had a broader base from which to live his faith and formulate his own creed.

> *The best way of knowing God is to love many things. Love that friend, that person, that thing, whatever you will like, you will be on the right path of knowing more thoroughly afterwards; that is what I say to myself. But you have to love with a high, with a serious and intimate sympathy, with a will, with intelligence, and you must always seek to know more thoroughly, better, and more. That is what leads to God, that leads to unshakeable faith.*
>
> —Cuesmes, between June 22 and 24, 1880

Vincent's transformation from a preacher of the word to an artist with a mission to serve humanity took place in the midst of the uncultured poor with whom he always remained connected in spirit. Through his art he aimed to highlight their worth and at the same time bring comfort and beauty into their dark impoverished huts. He had not given up his evangelical ambition. His restless soul and the intensity of his striving would continue to drive him forward onto his path of *loving many things,* from books to art, from poor peasants to pollard willows, wheat fields, irises, and sunflowers. He was free to explore ever deeper that to which he had innately responded and understood as a young boy and an art dealer-in-training, namely, that art and literature and religion were all paths that could *lead to God* and to *unwavering faith:*

> *What Rembrandt alone, or almost alone, has among painters, that tenderness in the gazes of human beings we see . . . in* The Jewish Bride. [It is] *that heartbroken tenderness, that glimpse of a superhuman infinite . . . one finds it in many places in Shakespeare.*
>
> —Saint-Rémy, July 2, 1889

His mission was to continue to live, to work, and to love the experiential way. His vocation was to use the language of Rembrandt to paint glimpses of *a superhuman infinite* for his own time and beyond. He remained a pilgrim with a will to hope, aspire, and search, never giving up his desire to create, remaining duty-bound to the work he had to do:

> *If I do nothing, if I don't study, if I don't keep on trying, then I'm lost, then woe betide me. That's how I see this, to keep on, keep on, that's what's needed.*
>
> —Cuesmes, between June 22 and 24, 1880

He believed wholeheartedly in his new path, hoping and trusting that Theo would too. For the freedom he gained by following his own creed made him, paradoxically, more dependent than ever before on the willingness of Theo to support him for the rest of his life.

Part II

Artist with a Mission

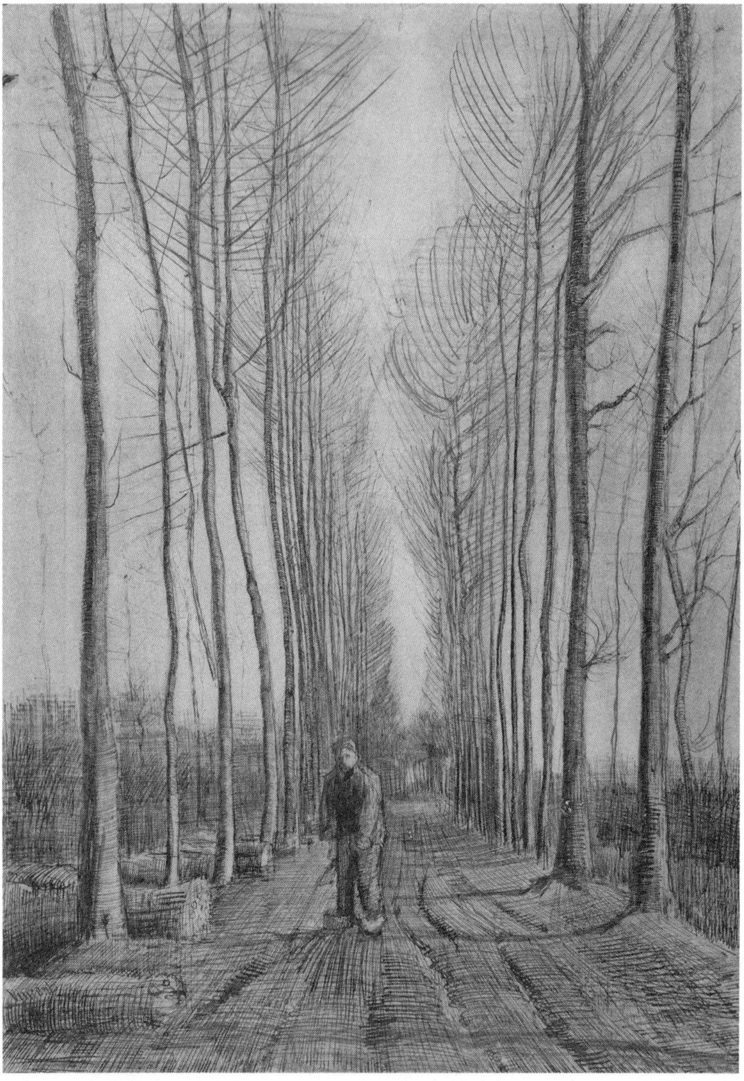

Avenue of Poplars. Nuenen: March 1884. Used with permission of the Van Gogh Museum, Amsterdam (Vincent van Gogh Foundation).

4

Etten: On the Artist's Path

Comparatively few people know why a draughtsman acts this way or that. But in general farmers and citizens suspect someone who looks for scenic spots or figures in all kinds of places, nooks and crannies, which others don't generally seek out, and accuse him of wickedness and evil intentions that have never entered his head. A peasant who sees me drawing an old tree trunk, and sees me sitting in front of it for an hour, thinks that I'm crazy, and of course laughs at me.

—Brussels, April 2, 1881

THE FIRST STEPS

For I am good for something after all, my life has a raison d'être!

—Cuesmes, between June 22 and 24, 1880

Vincent used a metaphor to describe his time in the Borinage. It had been like a molting period for birds. Birds go through a time when they shed their old feathers and grow new ones. He had also gone through such a period of transformation, and now confronted the choice, whether to stay there "in that time of molting," or:

to emerge from it as if renewed; but anyhow it must not be done in public, it is not at all amusing, it is not gay,

> *therefore, the best thing to do is to go into hiding. Well, so be it.*
>
> —Cuesmes, between June 22 and 24, 1880

With his decision to take up his pencil Vincent came out of hiding. His father was relieved that Vincent finally emerged from his time in the miner's hut, and he initially agreed to support Vincent's plans to practice his drawing skills in Brussels. With this kind of affirmation Vincent was able to make the first validated step onto his new vocational path. He installed himself in a small lodging house and began to work feverishly on copying prints by Millet and other artists. He also worked his way through exercises outlined in several drawing manuals. His aim at this time was to become an illustrator like those whose images he had admired in *The Graphic*. But his time in Brussels was brief. Pastor Van Gogh and Theo could not give him sufficient funds to support him, so there was no other alternative than for Vincent to return to his parental home, which now was in Etten, another little parish in the Brabant.

BACK IN THE PARSONAGE

> *Pa cannot empathize or sympathize with me, and I cannot function in Pa and Ma's routine, it makes me feel constrained—it suffocates me.*
>
> —Etten, on or about December 23, 1881

Vincent's parents noticed a big change in the prodigal son who appeared on the doorstep of their parsonage looking haggard and ill, almost a stranger. Vincent himself was very much aware that he had become *some sort of impossible and suspect character in the family* (Cuesmes, between June 22 and 24, 1880). He had developed a new sense of self through the experience and insights gained in the "university of misery." But he found it difficult to integrate his newfound beliefs into his parents' set ways. He was critical of institutional religion, as represented by their parish life. He became argumentative and defiant. His presence led to a state of continual disharmony in the otherwise settled rhythms of parsonage life. His views on many issues created disagreeable confrontations with his father, especially when they discussed the value of contemporary literature:

> *I do also read the Bible at times, just as I sometimes read Michelet or Balzac or Eliot, but in the Bible I see very different things than Pa and can't find what he draws from things based on his narrow academic way.*
>
> —Etten, on or about December 23, 1881

Vincent was convinced that the great themes in the Bible could also be found in present-day novels, where he had discovered stories of love, redemption, grace, and salvation. Both father and son had long and heated discussions in the parsonage study, which were disruptive and unsettling for Pastor Van Gogh. Vincent was emphatic, agreeing that *the Bible is eternal and everlasting,* but finding himself favoring and even savoring contemporary books. He wrote:

> [Jules Michelet] *gives such amazing, practical, and clear suggestions, easily applicable in this fast-paced frenzied modern life in which you and I find ourselves, that he helps us make progress fast, and we cannot do without him.*
>
> *And the Bible consists of layers and progressions. . . . For example, there is a difference between Moses and Noah on the one hand and Jesus and Paul on the other, and in my opinion Stowe and Michelet continue the Gospel, they do not repeat it.*

> *Take Michelet and Beecher Stowe: they don't say that the Gospel is not valid any longer, but they help us understand how applicable it is in this present age.*
>
> —Etten, November 23, 1881

Vincent tried to make his father understand that in certain novels the characters were truly human and compassionate and that some of the authors had much to teach. For example, Michelet *says things perfectly and out loud of which we merely find a germ in the Gospel, and Beecher-Stowe also goes as far as Michelet* (Etten, November 23, 1881). Many letters were written to Theo throughout his time in Etten to vent his frustration at not being able to convince his father of his views.

> *Now that the Rev. Ten Kate translated Goethe's Faust, Pa and Ma have read that book, for since a clergyman has translated it, it can't be all that indecent (now what is that???). However, they don't see anything in it but the disastrous consequence of an unchaste love. And they understand the Bible certainly just as poorly.*
>
> —Etten, on or about December 23, 1881

Several years later, even after his father's death, Vincent was still preoccupied with his failure to achieve the understanding and reconciliation he had hoped to find with him. In writing to his sister Willemien, he sought to bring their conflict to a close, at least for himself, by affirming that the Bible did remain the foundation for everything worthy in contemporary novels:

> *Do we have enough with the Bible? Nowadays I believe that Jesus himself would again say to those who just sit around full of melancholy, "It is not here, it is risen. Why seek ye the living among the dead?" If the spoken or written word is to remain the light of the world, then it is our right and our duty to recognize that we live in an age in which it is written in such a way, spoken in such a*

way to find something as great and equally as good and as original, and just as capable of overturning the whole old society as in the past; we can safely compare it with the old uprising by the Christians.

I, for my part, am always glad that I have read the Bible better than many people today, just because it gives me a certain peace that in the past there have been such high ideas. But just because I think the old is good, I find the new all the more so. All the more so because we ourselves can act in our own present time, and both the past and the future concern us only indirectly.

—Paris, late October 1887

DRAWING DEEP, DEEP IN THE HEART OF THE COUNTRY

Corot [French artist] *sketched and modeled every tree trunk with the same attention and love as if it were a human figure.*

—Etten, August 26, 1881

The more time I spend drawing the figure in particular, the more I find it a good thing because it also indirectly has a good influence on landscape drawing. If one draws a pollard willow as if it were a living being, which it actually really is, then, relatively speaking, the surroundings themselves follow, as long as one has concentrated one's efforts on that particular tree, and not given up until one has put some life into it.

—Etten, between October 12 and 15, 1881

Once again in rural Brabant, amid peasants working in the fields around Etten, Vincent regained his health. As he had in the Borinage, he continued to look to the ordinary experiences of life as the source for his *learning and observing,* but this time with a pen in hand, intent on mastering his drawing skills. Not surprisingly he brought to this task the same zeal and intensity with which he had approached his missionary work. His deep-rooted intimacy with the land of his childhood inspired him to declare himself an artist of peasant scenes. His new aim was to make drawings that revealed and celebrated the seasonal rhythms of rural life, the sowing and the reaping, the toil of peasants, the human connection with the soil. He felt that his own efforts were as crucial as the labors performed by the farmers in the fields. Wanting to prove to Theo that he was by no means idle, as he spent his days sketching and roaming through the landscape, he used the metaphor of a farmer's tool to describe his work:

> *I tell you what I tell myself: now more than ever, the time for action and energy has arrived. Therefore, put your hand to the plough! By being strong, one becomes strong. By believing, one learns to believe. By loving, one learns to love.*
>
> —Etten, November 19, 1881

Off he went on daily excursions, sketchpad and pens in hand, to observe the ploughmen drawing their own parallel lines on their earthen canvas. With intense concentration Vincent captured the figures of nameless laborers and the humble poor. In the spirit of the new realist art movement, he drew without pretense or affectation these people of the earth in their well-worn farming clothes, with sweat on their brow, working at their steadfast pace, doing an honest day's work. Vincent connected with the depth of their spirit and the fullness of their existence:

> *I have drawn five times over a man with a spade, a digger in fact, in all kinds of poses, twice a sower . . . and, finally, an old, sick farmer sitting on a chair by the hearth, with his head in his hands and his elbows on his knees. . . . I have to now continually draw diggers,*

> *sowers, plowers, men and women. I have to observe and draw everything that belongs to peasant life. Just like many others have done and are doing now. I no longer stand so helpless before nature, as I used to.*
>
> —Etten, mid-September, 1881

Aware that he was drawing on biblical imagery—the parables heard since his childhood—he repeatedly returned to the figures of sowers sowing their seeds. Works like Millet's "The Sower" further inspired him as he sought to highlight the intrinsic value and wholesomeness of rural life. Such drawings had a significant message; they were narratives about the foundations of life, the cyclical rhythms of life and death, the basic common ground of survival and health. Increasingly, Vincent felt he had found that "something to say that was really worth hearing." Was this not a continuation of missionary work? Hadn't his desire remained "to serve" humanity and to "be of use?" Could he translate his vision and his feelings into revelatory art, to bring those who labored hard to sustain life *before the eyes of the people?*

He himself was transformed by the new life force that compelled him to create. Sadly, his parents could not reconcile themselves with a son who could not, or would no longer, aspire to fulfill their expectations.

AIMER ENCORE

> *Life has become very dear to me, and I am very glad that I love. My life and my love are one. I tell you that I think it absolutely necessary to believe in God in order to be able to love. What I mean is, to believe in God is to feel that there is a God, not dead or on display, but a God who is alive, who with irresistible force urges us toward "aimer encore."*
>
> —Etten, November 23, 1881

During this time in Etten, Vincent fell in love with his cousin Kee Vos. She had recently been widowed and had brought her young son for a visit to the parsonage in Etten hoping that the new surroundings would provide some solace. Drawn to their suffering and the desire to offer consolation, Vincent spent hours in their company. Kee initially welcomed and responded to his kindness and thoughtfulness. But Vincent took her expressions of gratitude as a signal of her openness to a deeper relationship. But upon declaring his love and his hope for marriage, he was vehemently rejected. Kee took her child and fled the parsonage, back to her parents' home in Amsterdam. There ensued a period of futile attempts on Vincent's part to convince Kee and her parents that they were meant to marry. Repeatedly his family rebuked him for his persistence, and they eventually forbade him from further contact with Kee. But Vincent was stubborn. By now almost thirty, he did not want anything to stand in the way of his love for this (or, as it seemed, almost any) woman.

> *When I think of Kee, well, then I still say, "she and no other" . . . but it is not just recently that I have feelings for those women who are condemned and scorned by the clergymen, my love for them is even older than that for Kee Vos. Often when I walked the streets quite lonely and forlorn, half ill and miserable, without money in my pocket, I looked after them and envied the men who could go with them, and I felt as if those poor girls were my sisters, as far as our circumstances and life experiences were concerned. And see, it is an old feeling of mine that is deeply rooted. . . . But my feelings for Kee are quite new and something quite different. Without knowing it, she sits in a kind of prison. She too is poor and cannot do or let everything be as she wishes, and she feels a kind of resignation, and I think that the Jesuitism of clergymen and pious ladies often makes more of an impression on her than on me, a Jesuitism that no lon-*

> *ger impresses me because I have gotten to know some of their tricks. But she believes in them and could not bear it if the system of resignation, and sin, and God, and heaven knows what else, proved to be vain. And I believe it doesn't even occur to her that "God" actually maybe only begins when we say the word with which Multatuli ends his Prayer of an Unbeliever: "O God, there is no God!" Look, I find the God of the clergymen to be as dead as a doornail. But am I therefore an atheist? The clergymen consider me that—so be it—but look, I love, and how could I feel love if I did not live and others did not live, and then if we live, there is something full of wonder in that. Now call it God or human nature or whatever you want, but there is surely something which I cannot define with a system, even though it is very much alive and very real, and see, that is God for me, or as good as God.*
>
> —Etten, on or about December 23, 1881

In love, Vincent felt truly alive. His love was a force that energized and empowered him. It made him discover *a whole other hemisphere and feel the fullness and depth of life* (Etten, November 7, 1881). When Kee spurned his love he suffered long and deeply. With his whole being he had always yearned for an all-fulfilling love that could keep the fire in his soul alive. He eventually found another woman, one of his "sisters," to fill this need for a short time. But it was not until he surrendered himself completely to painting, discovering *the power of color in me that I did not possess before* (The Hague, August 14, 1882), that he could respond to that which was *very much alive and very real* and *as good as God*. Then he could truly say that his life and his love were one.

But now, in Etten, Vincent's persistent refusal to accept Kee's rejection and to adhere to his parents' admonition to stop pursuing her, resulted in deepening clashes with his family. Life in the parsonage became unbearable for everyone. By Christmas Day in 1881, Pastor Van Gogh ordered his son to leave his home. Once again, Vincent was on the road, this time carrying his bundle of art materials and a resolve to seek out other artists. He left for The Hague, hoping to find people there who *would understand that what I'm doing is driven by a deep feeling of a need for love* (The Hague, May 12 or 13, 1882). In The Hague there was a group of artists painting Dutch landscape scenes who belonged to The Hague School. His relative, the painter Anton Mauve, whom Vincent had visited on a previous short trip to The Hague, was one of them.

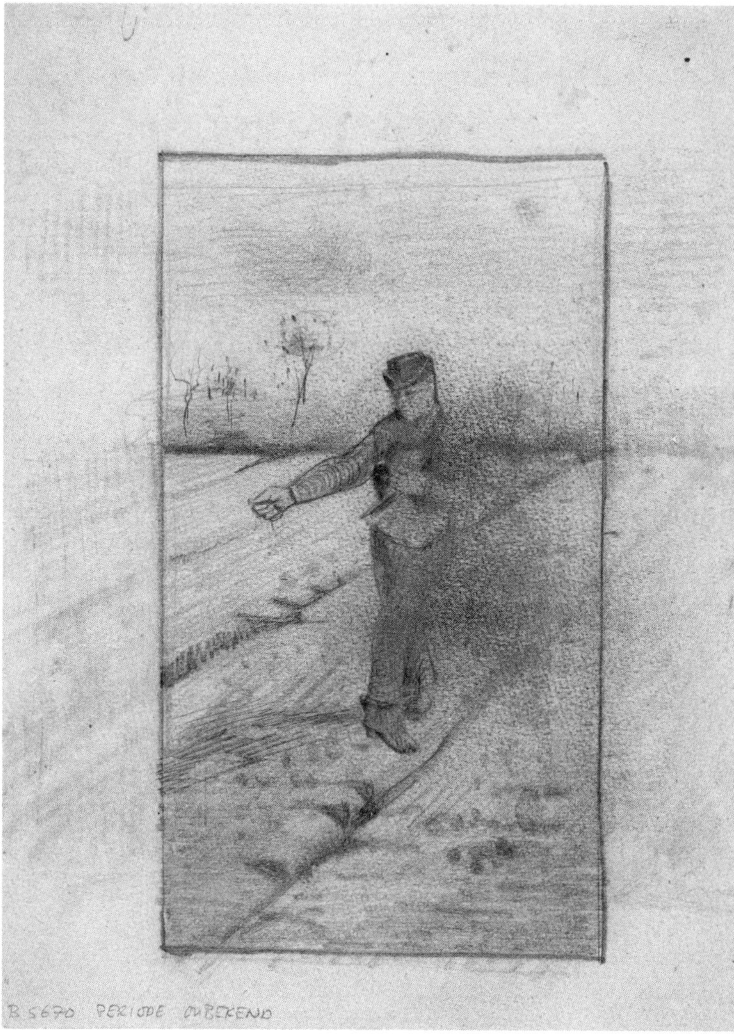

Sower. Etten: September 1881. Used with permission of the Van Gogh Museum, Amsterdam (Vincent van Gogh Foundation).

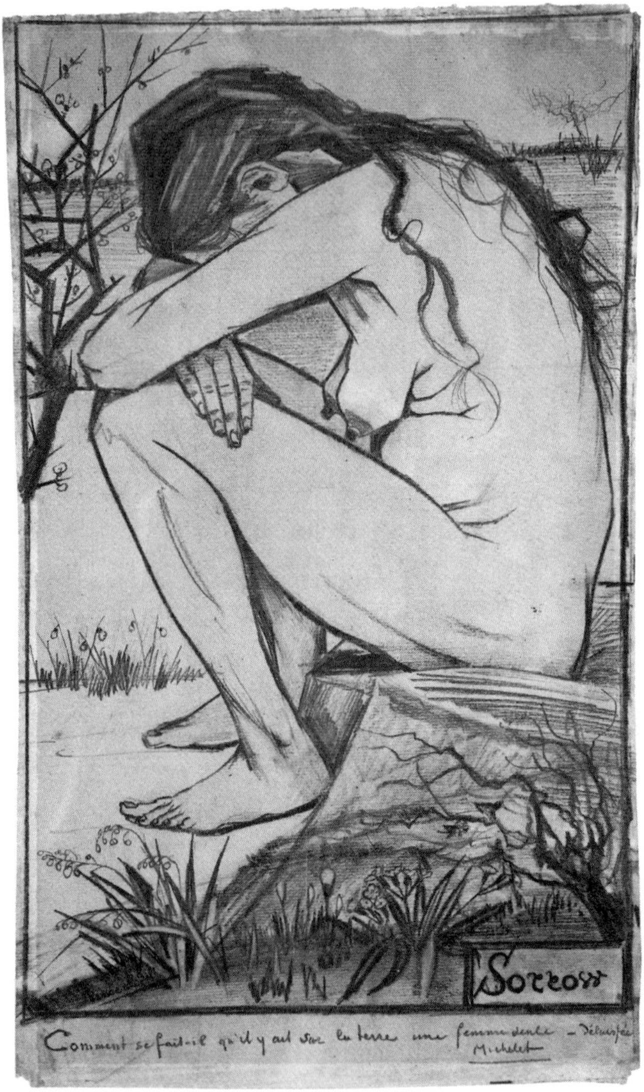

Sorrow. The Hague: April 10, 1882. Used with permission of The New Art Gallery Walsall, UK.

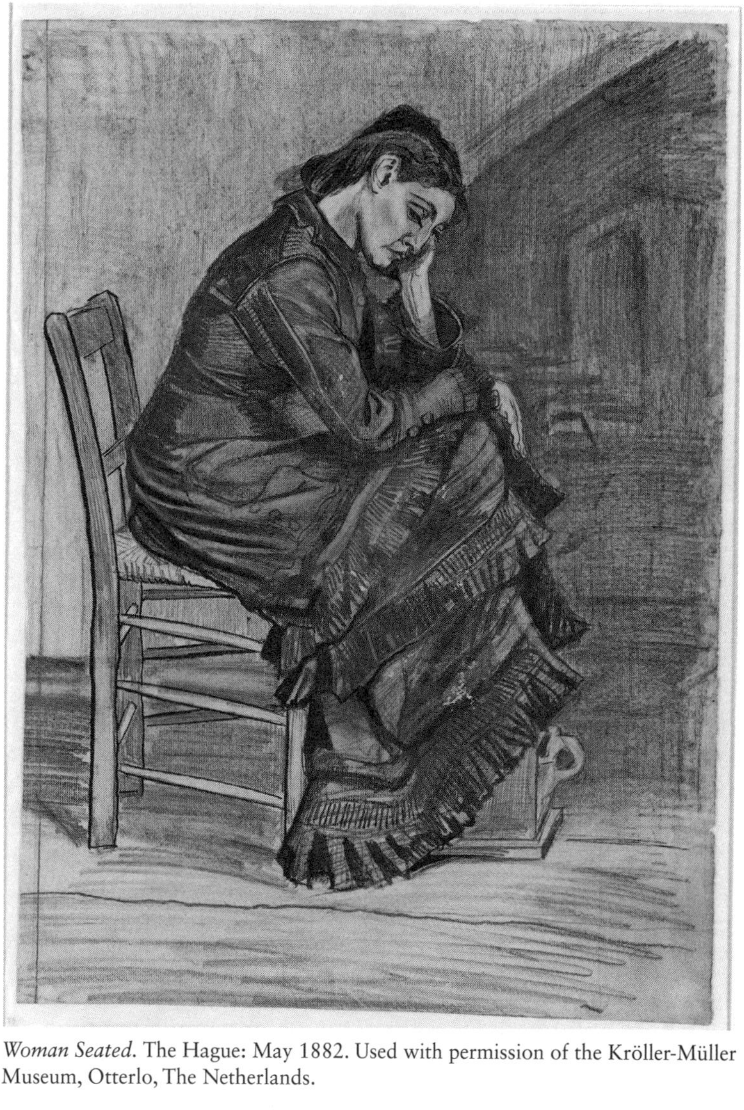

Woman Seated. The Hague: May 1882. Used with permission of the Kröller-Müller Museum, Otterlo, The Netherlands.

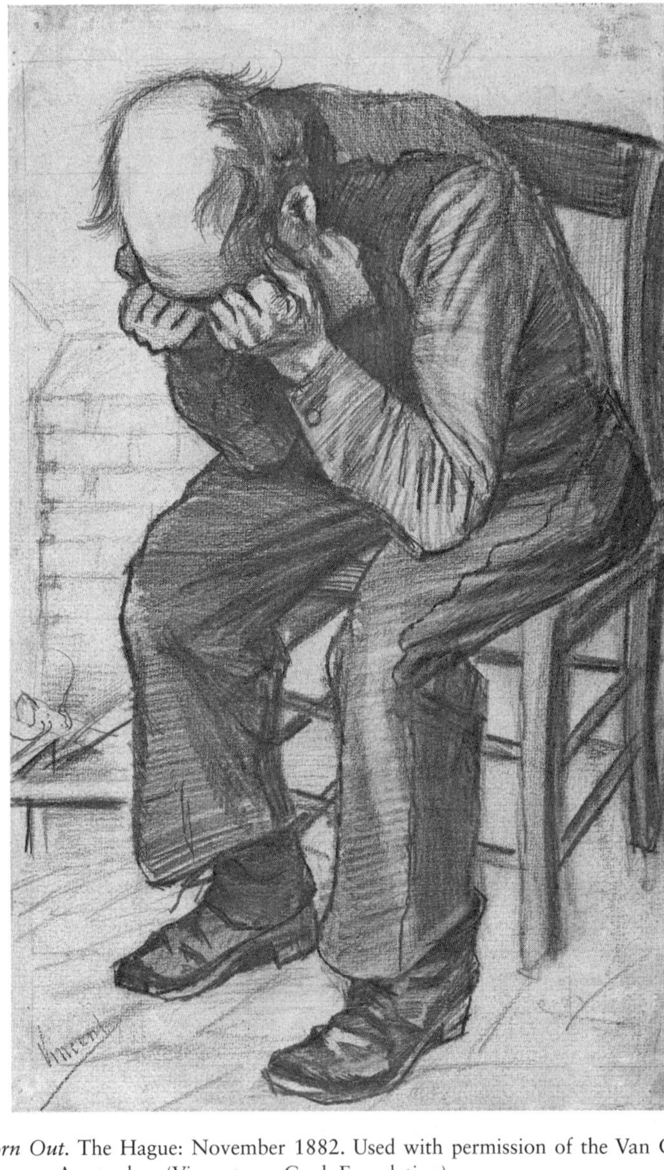

Worn Out. The Hague: November 1882. Used with permission of the Van Gogh Museum, Amsterdam (Vincent van Gogh Foundation).

5

The Hague: Something Serious

I now consider myself to be at the beginning of a beginning of making something serious.

—Etten, on or about December 23, 1881

Vincent was twenty-eight years old when he arrived in The Hague. He had practiced his drawing skills on his own for one year with very little encouragement or affirmation. Even his friends around Etten, the farmers who had modeled for him, didn't quite know what to make of his strange "scratches" on paper. Vincent craved some sort of mentorship and the companionships of colleagues who were as intent as he to draw from life. After his forced departure from Etten, Vincent arrived without warning on Anton Mauve's doorstep, not intending to visit but to stay. Mauve was initially supportive and hospitable. Fortunately, thanks to Theo's promise of a monthly stipend (the two brothers had by now formed an "art partnership"), Vincent found a small apartment to rent. Here, in his first true artist's studio, he would stay for almost two years.

AN ARTIST'S STUDIO—A REFUGE

"Blessed is he who has found his work," says Carlyle, and that's decidedly true. As for me, I say that I want to make figures from the people for the people, . . . making the drawings themselves preoccupies me the most. And thus, despite a feeling of dejection, the fact is that it

is wonderful to work on something that becomes more interesting the deeper you delve into it.

—The Hague, between December 13 and 18, 1882

Once he had equipped his studio in the small apartment on the Schenkweg, Vincent's great focus was on continuing to "delve into it"—to learn how to draw the human figure. That meant he had to find models. Since he could not afford the fees of professional models he had to look elsewhere for men and women willing to pose. He knew where to look. Inspired by the images he had seen in the London periodicals, he sought out suitable subjects in the almshouses, the third-class waiting rooms, and soup kitchens in the poorest parts of town. There, with the promise of a small fee, he found needy and lonely men and women to model for him. During such explorations he also discovered a yard full of laborers to be a worthy subject for his drawings: the equivalent of the peasants working in the lowly hovels of rural Brabant. Like peasants everywhere, these city laborers were struggling hard to make a living. Soon, a slow but steady trickle of almshouse men and women began to make their way to his modest apartment. Vincent came to think of his studio as a shelter for these poor folks where he could put into practice "loving your neighbor as yourself," thus satisfying his two desires—to draw from live models, and to comfort and care for the needy:

I can assure you of this: the work is going better the longer I'm at it and I feel, so to speak, more warmth of life as a result of it, and I think all the while constantly of you, since it's because of you that I'm able to work without significant obstacles, that is, without having my hands tied.

Sometimes the difficulties actually stimulate me. Now the time has still to come when we can put even more energy into the work. My ideal is to work with ever

> *more models, a whole flock of poor people for whom the studio could be a sort of harbor or refuge on cold days, or when they have no job or are in need. Where they know that there is a fire, and food, and drink, and a few quarters to be earned. It is only happening on a very small scale at the moment. I hope it will expand.*
>
> —The Hague, on or about April 2, 1883

Unaccustomed as they were to sitting in front of an intensely drawing man, it is unlikely that these men and women understood his motives. They came for the promise of respite, a moment beside a warm hearth, a few coins. But they also experienced something else—human warmth, respect, compassion, and a sense of worth. And aside from fulfilling his need for subjects, their presence filled Vincent's own need for companionship and love:

> *I believe that if one wants to make figures, one must have a warm feeling within oneself . . . a "good will to all," that is, one must have a real love for people. At least, I hope to try my best to be in such a mood as much as possible.*
>
> —The Hague, October 29, 1882

Vincent felt that the surest way to create good art was to penetrate deep into the nature of his subjects and discover their essence in *the poetry hidden in them* (The Hague, August 26, 1882). In order to do this he had to identify with his models, to become like one of them. Thus he did just as he had done with the miners in the Borinage: he entered into their experience. As a missionary, he had gained access into the depths of his own struggles and his own nature by identifying fully with the despair of a suffering person. Vincent did not just look *at* his models in order to draw them. He aimed to see as they saw, to feel as they felt. He looked below the surface of appearances and found there something that was invisible to the eyes of most other people:

> [My] *work lies in the heart of the people, that I must keep myself close to the ground, that I must delve deeply into life and make progress despite great cares and difficulties. I can't imagine any other way.*
>
> —The Hague, May 12 or 13, 1882

This combination, early in his career, of two great passions—to draw and to serve the poor—prepared him to become a particular kind of artist. His artistic and life's purpose would be to unite with the soul of the other. He did this with destitute persons but then carried this soul-uniting work into solidarity with all life, whether in the form of a wheat field, a pollard willow, a sunflower, or a star-lit sky:

> *Through working a lot . . . I hope to make something good one day. I haven't got it yet, but I'm hunting after it and fighting for it. I want something serious, something fresh—something which will have a soul in it! Onward, onward.*
>
> —The Hague, January 3, 1883

For now, however, Vincent's art was founded in his solidarity with the poor, whose hardships he shared. Like his models, he was constantly in need of money, never having enough to eat, always lonely and often homesick. At times, sketching from life people who were often as miserable as he was made his work almost unbearably difficult. Vincent had read a biography about Millet where the artist was supposed to have cried out "*L'art c'est un combat!*" (Art is a battle). Though he identified with this sentiment, he was also encouraged by Millet's example of perseverance to remain true to his art despite the "battle":

> *I do not have any great plans for the future; for a moment I may feel rising within me the desire for a care-free life, for success—each time I go fondly back to the trouble,*

> *the cares, to a difficult life—and think, it is better this way, I learn more from it, it does not debase me, it is not on this road one perishes.*
>
> —The Hague, May 12 or 13, 1882

Vincent looked upon his models as people who had something to teach him about life. If he could render them in all honesty in his drawings, they would someday show others how even a poor, old, ugly, or unhappy person had, through life's experience and sorrow, attained a mind and a soul. He exclaimed to Theo, *Do you realize that it's so very highly necessary that honest people should remain in art*? (The Hague, between December 4 and 9, 1882). His drawings had to reveal that these people were real, that they lived in real places, in cities and villages nearby, in everyone's neighborhoods. Such drawings would *touch some people* and encourage the response of "loving your neighbor as yourself."

PASSION FOR ART AND BOOKS

> *If you now can forgive a man for deepening his study of paintings, admit also that the love of books is as sacred as the love of Rembrandt—I even think that the two are complementary. . . . I am just as fond of Sydney Carton in Dickens'* Tale of Two Cities, *and I could show you other figures as strangely outstanding in other books, with a more or less striking resemblance . . . like . . . Kent, a character in* King Lear *by Shakespeare. My God, how beautiful he is* [Shakespeare]*! Who is as mysterious as he is? His language and style is quite equal to an artist's brush, trembling with fever and emotion. But one must learn to read, just as one must learn to see and learn to live.*
>
> —Cuesmes, between June 22 and 24, 1880

Besides sketching, writing numerous lengthy letters, and taking long walks, Vincent gave in to his irresistible passion for books and his constant need *to educate myself, to study, if you like, just as much as I want to eat my bread* (Cuesmes, between June 22 and 24, 1880). In The Hague he gravitated to the novels by realist authors such as Charles Dickens, Guy de Maupassant, Victor Hugo, George Eliot, and Emile Zola. These novels, written in the mid- to late-1800s exposed the harsh realities of life, focusing on violence, prejudice, and corruption. Each novel or story in its own way dealt with a universal reality of lives threatened by poverty. Yet, they also highlighted strength, endurance, hope, and the redemptive qualities of the human spirit. The stories revealed to the literate public the vast population of the urban and rural poor who struggled, under the circumstances of the Industrial Revolution, to make their living in abysmal conditions. These novels reflected the same circumstances depicted in the illustrations of *The Graphic* and the paintings by Daumier, Millet, Courbet, and other contemporary artists. The hope of many of these authors and artists was that public awareness, aroused by the plight of the working poor, would lead to social reforms and justice.

The great literary works of the time and the graphic art depicting the conditions of laborers hugely impacted Vincent's outlook on life. Through constant reading and observation, he entered into the written and painted stories and "befriended" the fictional characters. The narratives wove themselves into Vincent's thought patterns, influencing his actions and inspiring him in his own sketching of the rural and urban poor. Vincent's drawings themselves became illustrative commentaries on the times. The men and women who modeled for him in his studio walked right out of the pages of Dickens's stories and the illustrations of *The Graphic:*

> *For me the English draughtsmen are what Dickens is in the field of literature. It is the same sentiment, noble and healthy, and to which one always returns.*
>
> —The Hague, on or about September 19, 1882

He read with great passion all the novels of Emile Zola, whose realistic characters experienced drama and passion in the streets of Paris. From the authors he studied he took to heart their lessons about life and faith. In Victor Hugo he found an especially wise and faith-filled man who wrote about religious ideas, relating them to the present times of cultural upheaval and unrest. It was from Victor Hugo that he found the reference to "something on high"—the naming of a divine power greater than oneself—an idea Vincent could relate to. Having separated himself from the religious institutions and especially from the pious religion and language of his father, he was often at a loss to describe his intuition of a power beyond the material world. He referred to Hugo's term in many of his letters:

> *You know* Les Misérables, *don't you?—and no doubt the illustrations Brion drew for it—very good and convincing. It's good to read a book like that once again, it seems to me, just to keep some feelings and moods alive, that is, the love of man above all, and of faith in and consciousness of something higher, namely of the something on high.*
>
> —The Hague, on or about March 29 and April 1, 1883

He referred to the "something on high" when he wrote about sketches he had made of an old man from the almshouse. He felt that a sketch like this could portray visibly something as inexpressible as a spiritual reality, the inexplicable sense of a "rayon d'en haut" ("A ray from on high," another expression from Hugo) (Amsterdam, April 3, 1878):

It seems to me to be a painter's duty to try to put a thought into his work. In this print I was trying to express this, but I can't say it as beautifully, as strikingly as it is in reality, of which this is only a faint reflection seen in a dark mirror—that it seems to me that one of the strongest proofs for the existence of "something on high" in which Millet believed, namely in a God and in an eternity, is the inexpressibly moving quality seen in the expression of an old man like that, perhaps without his being aware of it, as he sits so quietly in the corner by his hearth. At the same time, something dignified, something noble, that can't be destined for the worms.

This is far removed from any theology, just simply the fact that the poorest little woodcutter or farmer on the heath or miner can have moments of emotion and mood which give him a sensation of feeling close to an eternal home. . . .

There is something indescribable in those aspects—all of nature seems to speak; and when one goes home, one has the same feeling as having finished reading a book by Victor Hugo, for instance. As for me, I cannot understand why everybody does not see it and feel it—after all, nature or God does it for everyone who has eyes and ears and a heart to understand. It seems to me that the reason a painter is happy is because, once he is able to render some of what he sees, he is in harmony with nature. And that is important, one knows what one has to do, there is an abundance of subjects, and as Carlyle rightly says, "blessed is he who has found his work."

If that work—like that of Millet, Dupre, Israels, etc.—has as its objective to bring peace, namely to say "sursum corda," to lift up your heart to heaven, then it is

> *doubly stimulating. One is then also less lonely, because one thinks, "It's true I'm sitting here alone, but while I am sitting here holding my tongue, my work will perhaps speak to my friend, and whoever sees it will not suspect me of being coldhearted."*
>
> —The Hague, November 26 and 27, 1882

When Vincent explained to Theo his intention of making a sketch of an old man saying grace before a meal, he wrote that it was to express the special religious mood of Christmas and New Year in Holland and England, where celebratory customs were still animated by faith. He admitted feeling the need for such religious celebrations and missed the opportunity to participate in them. And even though he had distanced himself from his religious upbringing, he was nevertheless grounded in a faith that had its beginnings in a home where the rituals and customs of the church year were joyfully anticipated:

> *I now have two more drawings: one is of a man reading the Bible and the other is of a man saying grace before his midday meal, which is on the table. Both are decidedly done in what one might call an old-fashioned sentiment—they are the same type of figures as the one of the little old man with his head in his hands. . . .*
>
> *My intention with these two and with the first little old man is one and the same, namely to express the unique mood of Christmas and New Year. In Holland and in England, there is always still something of a worshipful sentiment. . . . Whether or not one exactly agrees with the form it takes, it is something one respects if there is a sincere feeling in it, and I for my part can fully share in it and even feel a need for it, at least in so far as I have the same feelings—just like that a little old man—for a belief in something on high, even though I don't quite know who or what will be there.*

> *I like what Victor Hugo said: les religions passent—mais Dieu demeure* [religions pass, but God remains]. *And then I also find it good what Gavarni said: Il s'agit de saisir ce qui ne passe pas dans ce qui passe* [the point is to grasp what does not pass away in what does pass away]. *And one of the things "qui ne passerons pas"* [that will not pass away] *is the "quelque chose la-haut"* [something on high] *and the belief in God, even though the forms may change, such a change is as necessary as the renewal of greenery in the spring. But you will understand from all this that in these drawings it wasn't my intention to pay homage to the form but rather to show that I greatly respect the Christmas and New Year sentiment.*
>
> *And if I succeeded in showing any sentiment or expression, it is because I myself feel it.*
>
> —The Hague, between December 13 and 18, 1882

Vincent's letters abound with references to art and artists, authors and stories. When he took his long walks through city streets or on country lanes, he continued to give painterly descriptions of all that he saw. More often than not, the mood of a landscape or the scene of workmen digging up a road were linked to artwork and stories. Walking beyond the city walls helped him escape the narrow confines of the streets of The Hague. He did this as often as he could to satisfy his longing for nature.

In one long letter, he wrote how he walked to a beach in Scheveningen (an outskirt of The Hague) and how he found lots of cornfields, adding, however, that they were not as beautiful as those in the Brabant. But seeing the fields assured him that there had to be sowers, and reapers, and gleaners—all these laborers of the soil that he missed in city life. He needed to see them, to be among them, or at least to be in places where their toil was evident; such scenes were as necessary as breathing! And he needed, just as much, to be fed by the artworks he loved. Describing a stand of wind-blown, bronze-green bushes between the village and the sea made him exclaim, *Oh, now this is Ruisdael's Bush.* Ever since Vincent had seen Jacob van Ruisdael's paintings in the Louvre in his days as an apprentice art dealer, he was captivated by this artist's ability to express the real drama of nature. On many occasions he had written to Theo how he had the mysterious sense of walking through a Ruisdael landscape. Such an outing to the beach at Scheveningen nourished him on several levels: the physical exertion of his rigorous walk, the yearning to breathe in the wholesomeness of rural life, and the sensation that he was in the presence of artists he admired. It all stirred him to set up his easel on the beach, moving it as the tide came closer, and sketching the dunes, the bushes, and the grass. And when he sat down to write to Theo in the evenings, he included small "scratches" of his sketches amidst his verbal descriptions. This way his brother could participate in the whole experience on more than one level, too:

> *See, this is a scratch of the little path down to the sea. I thought of you especially on that walk. I don't doubt that you will agree with me that the dunes in the vicinity of the city and Scheveningen have lost much of what was real in the last ten years. . . . At that time things were more Ruisdael-like than they are now. If one wants to see something that brings to mind a Daubigny, a Corot-like mood, one must go further to where the ground is almost untouched by the footsteps of bathers . . . well, I found the virginity of nature to be outstanding on the walk I told you about. . . .*
>
> *Seldom in these times has the silence, has nature alone, spoke to me like this. Sometimes it is precisely these places where one no longer feels anything of what is known as the civilized world and has decidedly turned one's back on it. Sometimes it is precisely in these places that one needs to find tranquility. Only I would have*

> *wished you to be here, too, because you, I believe, would have had the same impression of finding yourself in surroundings just like I imagine Scheveningen was at the time when the first Daubignys appeared.*
>
> —The Hague, July 29 and 30, 1883

The memory of work by artists and authors he admired continued to accompany him wherever he went, always inspiring his own creative work, whether writing, drawing, or painting.

A FORSAKEN CREATURE

> *Which is the more civilized, sensitive, manly—*
> *to leave a woman or to care for a forsaken one?*
>
> —The Hague, on or about May 7, 1882

Vincent had his two passions: to draw from living figures and to minister, following the example of Jesus. Both these passions led him to bring one of his models, a woman called Sien, into his studio apartment to stay. Destitute and sick, she had a little daughter and was pregnant with another child. Vincent was once again drawn to the misery of a woman, one in this case who epitomized the images in *The Graphic* and the destitute people who populated the stories of Dickens, Zola, Eliot, and Hugo:

> *This winter I met a pregnant woman, who was abandoned by the man whose child she was carrying. A pregnant woman who roamed the streets in winter—having to earn her bread, you can imagine how.*
>
> *I took that woman as a model and worked with her the whole winter. I could not give her the full daily wage of a model, but rather I paid her rent and have been able until now, thank God, to save her and her child from hunger and cold by sharing my own bread*

> *with her. When I met this woman, she caught my attention because she looked ill. I let her use the baths and as many fortifying tonics as I could afford. She's become much healthier. I went with her to Leiden, where there's a maternity hospital for the confinement of women. . . .*
>
> *It seems to me that any man who is as valuable as the leather in his shoes would have done the same in such circumstances. I find what I did so simple and self-evident that I thought I could keep it to myself.*
>
> —The Hague, on or about May 7, 1882

Theo's hard-earned money, of which he sent a portion to Vincent every month, was now also to be spent taking care of Sien, her daughter, and another expected child. Yet he felt attached to her, and not just because she was a faithful model. They were two unhappy people keeping each other company, carrying each other's burdens, making the unbearable bearable:

> *There is nothing special about her, except that she is just an ordinary woman from the people who, for me, have something of the sublime. Whoever loves one ordinary common person and is beloved by her is already happy, despite the dark side of life. If she had not needed relief this winter, the bond between her and me would not have been formed after the circumstances of my disappointment and wounded love. In fact, it was the feeling of being useful after all, in spite of that disappointment, which brought me to myself again and made me revive. It is not that I looked for it, but I found it; and now it is a fact that there is a warm affection between her and me, and it would not do me good to give that up.*
>
> —The Hague, June 1 and 2, 1882

When Theo announced his visit to The Hague to meet Sien, Vincent hoped to convince him that caring for her was the right thing to do. He turned to the characters of a story by Zola called "Le Ventre de Paris" (The Belly of Paris) to speak on his behalf:

> *Now I do have to ask you what you think of Mme. François, who picks up poor Florent who lies unconscious in the middle of the road along which the vegetable carts are passing, and lets him ride with her. Although the other vegetable sellers shout: "Let him lie there, the drunk! We have no time to pick men up lying in the gutter," &c. The character of Mme François stands out in the background of the Halles throughout the whole book, in contrast to the brutal egoism of the other women, so calm and so worthy and so sympathetic.*
>
> *See, Theo, I for one believe that Mme. François' act showed true humanity, and concerning Sien, I have done and will do what I believe someone like Mme. François would have done for Florent if he had not been concerned more about politics than about her. So there it is, and that humanity is the salt of life, without that I would not care about life. . . . I already spoke a few words about the humanity which a person may possess, for example, Mme. François in the book by Zola. However, I have no compassionate plans or thoughts, as if I could do the same for everyone. But I'm not ashamed to say (though I know very well that the word compassion is out of favor) that, I for my part, have always felt the need to love one creature or another, and will continue to do so. Preferably, though I don't know why, an unfortunate or forsaken or abandoned creature. I once nursed a badly burnt miner for six weeks or two months, I shared my food with an old man for a whole winter, and I don't know what else, and now Sien. But I do not believe to this day that this was foolish or bad. I*

> *see it as being so natural and self-evident that I cannot understand that people can in general be so indifferent to each other. Let me add that if I was wrong, you also did wrong in helping me so faithfully—it would be too absurd if this were wrong. I have always believed that "love thy neighbor as thyself" is no exaggeration but a normal condition.*
>
> —The Hague, July 23, 1882

Sharing life with Sien was not easy. Looking after her needs meant that he had less time for his drawing. His health suffered, too. He was exhausted and because he stretched the little food he had to feed Sien and her daughter, he was constantly undernourished. While Vincent was making arrangements with the maternity hospital for the birth of Sien's child, he himself succumbed to his weakness and had to be hospitalized. Yet, once Sien had given birth, he neglected his own healing and hurried to be by her side. Upon entering the maternity ward, Vincent was overcome with emotion to see Sien resting next to the tiny baby asleep in its cradle. It was the miracle of the Nativity! It was a scene such as Rembrandt had painted! It was Rembrandt's print come to life—the image that had hung in his father's study years ago. Vincent shared this moment with Theo:

> *It is a strong and powerful emotion which seizes a person when he sits beside the woman he loves with a little child in the cradle next to them. And even though it was only a hospital where she lay and where I sat by her, it is always the eternal poetry of the Christmas night with the little child in the stable, just as the old Dutch painters interpreted it, and Millet and Breton—that light in the darkness—a brightness shining in the midst of a dark night. So I then hung the big etching by Rembrandt up on the wall, the two women by the cradle where one reads from the Bible by the light of a candle while the large shadows create a chiaroscuro effect in*

> *the whole room. I have hung a few other prints there too, . . .* Christus Consolator *by Scheffer, . . .* The Sower *and* The Diggers *by Millet,* The Bush *by Ruysdael.*
>
> —The Hague, July 6 and 7, 1882

He brought Sien and her baby back to his little apartment and helped her regain her strength. Initially, Vincent sent descriptions to Theo of how moved he was to witness the tenderness with which Sien nursed her child. Such scenes had always touched him. Now more than ever they became models for his drawings in a place that was:

> *not a mystical or mysterious art studio, but one that has rooted itself in the fullness of life, a studio with a cradle, a baby's potty, where there is no stagnation, but everything pushes and urges and stirs to activity. . . .*
>
> *For me it is as clear as daylight that one must feel what one draws, that one must live in the reality of family life if one wishes to render the intimacy of that family life: a mother with her child, a washerwoman, a seamstress, whatever it may be. Through persistent practice the hand gradually learns to obey that feeling. But if I should extinguish that feeling and the powerful desire to have my own household—that would be suicide. That is why I say, "en avant"* [onward], *despite dark shadows, cares, and difficulties.*
>
> —The Hague, July 6, 1882

He wrote about his relationship with Sien, about how much they benefited one another, convincing himself that this little family surrounding him was some kind of ideal. His yearning for a nurturing family to call his own made him desperate to hold these bits of broken humanity together. He had been deeply influenced by ideals of charity, by the biblical parables, and contemporary novels and art. He wanted his own family life to resemble the touching and humble scenes of families around the hearth, of women sitting by the side of a cradle, mending and knitting, or peeling potatoes—scenes that had always uplifted and comforted him. Vincent drew such images of Sien, drawing art from reality, just as he searched for and found real life expressed through art:

> *And through the children she* [Sien] *deals with reality and is learning to cope by herself. For me, books and reality and art are alike. I would find anyone who was out of touch with real life annoying, but somebody who is fully in the midst of it has knowledge of it and feels independently. If I did not look for art in real life, I might find her stupid; as it is, I wish things were different, but after all, I am content with the way things are.*
>
> —The Hague, February 11, 1883

Vincent intended to marry Sien. He spent countless hours trying to persuade Theo that he could not do otherwise. He found, once again, affirmation of his actions in the stories he was reading. Theo was at this time also caring for a woman in need:

> *When I read your letter this morning I was very touched by what you wrote. Those are the things of which the world sometimes says, "Why should he interfere with that?" And yet it isn't so much our own deed but rather the circumstances that compel us to act. And once we have understood the situation, such a deep and bottomless pity is aroused in us that we no longer hesitate.*
>
> *And I believe this is the case with you, and what can I say other than that it seems to me that in such cases we must follow our impulses? Victor Hugo says, "Over and above reason there is conscience." There are things that we feel to be good and true, although from the point of view of reason and calculation there is much that is inexplicable and obscure. And although the society in which we live considers such actions as thoughtless or reckless or foolish or I don't know what all, what can*

> *we say once the hidden forces of compassion and love have been awakened deep inside us?*
>
> —The Hague, on or about January 10, 1883

Vincent took literally the words of the Gospel, "Bear one another's burdens and so fulfill the law of Christ" (Galatians 6:2), asking Theo, *how far may one go in becoming involved with an unfortunate woman?* and answering his own rhetorical question: *ad infinitum* (The Hague, on or about April 11, 1883). It seemed most natural for him to take upon himself the welfare of a woman who was not his wife and children who were not his own. Yet, he knew that in his plan to marry Sien he would face strong familial objections; he especially worried that his bond with Theo would break *over the woman.* In reality, it was his relationship with Sien that began to deteriorate. Sien was not as gentle and complacent as Vincent had depicted her. Her rough life had shaped her character. Her demeanor was coarse. The birth of the baby boy did not soften her. Vincent defended her by saying that she hadn't known what was good, so how could she be good? But he was worn out and discouraged. He had sought to do the right thing as a matter of faith. And he had justified his actions by assuring himself that his life with Sien would also inspire the production of art, which, by its sheer honesty, would become saleable in time. But that was not the case. By Christmas of his second year in The Hague, he reached a very low point. He reread Dickens' Christmas stories of redemption and reconciliation. But the hope and grace found in *The Christmas Carol* was elusive in his relationship with Sien. Mindful that the artist's path was a "battle," he pushed on. He kept drawing, he went for long walks, he cared for Sien and the children, he tended his household as best he could, and he wrote long letters, feeling despite it all:

> *a power in me that I must develop, a fire that I may not put out, but must encourage, even though I do not know*

> *to what outcome it will lead me, and would not be surprised if it were a dreary one.*
>
> *How much good it does a person who is in a somber mood to walk on the empty beach and to look at the grayish-green sea with the long white streaks of the waves. But if one feels the need of something grand, something infinite, something in which one can know God, one does not need to go far to find it. I thought I saw something deeper, more infinite, more eternal than the ocean in the expression of the eyes of a little child when it wakes in the morning, and coos or laughs because it sees the sun shining into its cradle. If there is a "rayon d'en haut"* [a ray from above], *perhaps one can find it there.*
>
> —The Hague, December 10, 1882

While in his drawings of Sien and her child he pursued an art "rooted in life," his idealization of *the way things are* clashed constantly with the real life of misery. *Life and reality have left its mark* (Etten, on or about December 23, 1881) on Sien, and although he did look into her face *with endless sympathy*, it wasn't an easy reality to live with. This art and life that he was weaving together had pulled him into his own work of art, so to speak, where he no longer had enough strength to uplift and save. Still, he was driven by compassion, by faith, and by the expressive power inherent in art and literature to respond to the needs of the world. In this "tableaux vivant" (living picture) of a mother beside the cradle, he found the expression of "a forsaken creature" whom he might transform through his compassion and love.

THE PERSONAL BECOMES UNIVERSAL

> *I could not draw Sorrow if I did not feel it myself.*
>
> —The Hague, on or about April 14 1882

> *Try to understand that your model is NOT your final aim, but the means of giving form and strength to your thought and inspiration.*
>
> —Quoted from Dickens, The Hague, November 5, 1882

> *I want something more concise, more simple, more serious; I want more soul and more love and more heart.*
>
> —The Hague, on or about December 11, 1882

Vincent made many sketches of Sien culminating in the most simple, yet most expressive drawing of all—"Sorrow." With a single contour line Vincent succeeded in expressing *something about the struggle of life.* Vincent had not abstracted the female body, but eliminated any unnecessary detail so that the focus on the expressive quality of Sien's pose became more evident. He knew Sien so well and drew her reality so faithfully that he was able to render her figure as an intensely personal image of forlorn sadness, at the same time highlighting an emotion that became universally understood. Vincent's drawing transcended the real life predicament of the woman posing before him. Through this drawing, Sien became more than an ordinary individual with a harsh lot in life; she was an image of human sorrow. Victor Hugo achieved the same collectively understood characterization in his description of the prostitute Fantine in *Les Misérables.* She too embodied the essence or the type of a woman living in utter misery:

> *I am in the process of reading the last part of* Les Misérables. *The figure of Fantine, a prostitute, made a deep impression on me. Oh, I know that in reality one will not find precisely the same Fantine, but this character described by Hugo—like all his characters for that matter—is true, because it is the essence of what one sees in reality. It is the type of which one only meets individuals.*
>
> —The Hague, on or about April 11, 1883

By having entered into an intentional solidarity with Sien, Vincent had learned to truly see below the surface of things. The hand holding his pencil transformed Sien's pose into the *essence of what one sees in reality* (The Hague, on or about April 11, 1883), the visible that alluded to the invisible.

From elements in the landscape, Vincent also created expressive drawings, which he related to human emotions. His associative manner of thinking had him constantly compare subjects in nature with human characteristics. On his walks through the countryside he saw, for example, *expression and a soul* in trees (The Hague, December 10, 1882). He once compared a row of pollard willows to a row of almshouse men lining up at a soup kitchen. He felt that young corn had something so pure and gentle about it that it gave him the same emotional sensation as if he were looking at the expression of a child asleep in its cradle. And in a clump of twisted roots clinging to the earth he found a metaphor for human suffering and struggle:

> *Now, I've tried to put into the landscape the same sentiment as shown in the figure: through, as it were, a convulsively and passionately clinging to the earth and yet being half torn up by the storm. I wanted, both in that white slender female figure and in the gnarled black roots with their knots, to express something about the struggle of life. Or rather, because I tried, without any philosophizing, to be faithful to nature that I saw before me, almost inadvertently both express something of that great struggle.*
>
> —The Hague, May 1, 1882

The images Vincent created had to have significant narrative qualities. They had to speak to the soul of the viewer without the necessity of words. In order to be universally understood, they had to be straightforward and simple. Vincent described a painting by Mauve that showed a fishing boat drawn up to the dunes by a tired horse. He continued to describe those old, poor, and ill-treated "nags" who stood there, patient, submissive, willing, resigned, and quiet, waiting to finish pulling up the heavy boats. They did it year in, year out, without complaining. This image, he felt, spoke more effectively about the subject of "resignation" than any pastor's sermon.

> *This is THE resignation, the real kind, not that of the clergymen. I find such a mighty deep, practical, silent philosophy in this painting. It seems to say, "Knowing how to suffer without complaining, that is the only practical thing, it is there one finds the great science, the lesson to learn, the solution of the problem of life." I think that this painting by Mauve would be one of the rare paintings before which Millet would remain standing a long time, and mutter to himself, "Il a du coeur ce peintre-la"* [this painter has a heart].
>
> —The Hague, March 11, 1882

To make his language as simple as possible, Vincent had to create images that were implicitly symbolic, like a worn-out "nag" plodding along the canal, that could convey the feeling of resignation. In order to see that *all reality is at the same time symbolic* (Nuenen, October 1885), an artist had to become deeply involved with observing nature, for it was *the painter's duty to be entirely absorbed by nature and to use all his intelligence to express sentiment in his work so that it becomes intelligible to other people* (The Hague, July 31, 1882). To his friend Anton Rappard, he emphasized that in order to draw a subject the artist had to feel it deeply within himself and know it intimately (Nuenen, on or about March 13, 1884). He had to engage in a hand-to-hand struggle with nature before he could expect any success in his work. Once he knew his subject well Vincent could transform it into his art language, his shorthand that could distill the essence of the everyday ordinary things onto his canvas:

> *I go and sit with a white board before the place that strikes me; I look at what is before my eyes; I say to myself, this white board must become something; I come back, dissatisfied; I put it aside, and after I have rested a little, feeling kind of fearful, I take a look at it; then I still feel dissatisfied because I have that beautiful nature scene too much in my mind for me to feel satisfied; and yet, I see in my work an echo of what struck me. I see that nature has told me something, has spoken to me and that I have written it down in shorthand. In my shorthand there may be words that cannot be deciphered—errors or omissions—yet something is there of what the wood or beach or figure have said.*
>
> —The Hague, September 3, 1882

After observing and studying the scenes before him long enough, his shorthand became iconographic for nature's voice. He stood before her in a receiving mode, letting the images imprint themselves on his soul; within him the "heard" and the seen were transformed, like the philosopher's stone, into something else: lines, shapes, colors, movement, balance, texture. The resulting image on paper or canvas mirrored the observed, "giving form and strength to his thoughts and inspiration"; it was nature seen through the lens of an artist's soul. Vincent knew that his two drawings, "Sorrow" and "Roots," were not pieces that would in a general way appeal to the public. But he was compelled to make such drawings from life, hoping that Theo would understand his conception of art:

> *To arrive at the truth, one must work long and hard. What I want and set as my goal is damned difficult, and yet I don't believe I aim too high. I want to create drawings that touch some people. "Sorrow" is a small beginning, perhaps such little landscapes as "Laan von Meerdervoort," "Rijswijk Meadows," and "Fish Drying*

Barn" are also a small beginning. In those there is at least something straight from my own emotions. Whether it is in figures or in landscapes, I do not want to express some sentimental melancholy but serious sorrow.

In short, I want to progress so far in my work that people will say, "That man feels deeply and that man feels tenderly, despite my so-called coarseness, you understand—maybe precisely because of it. It may seem pretentious to talk like this now, but that is also the reason why I want to push on.

What am I in the eyes of most: a nonentity or an eccentric or a disagreeable man, someone who has no position in society and will not have one, in short a little lower than the lowest.

Well then, if this were exactly like that, then through my work I'd like to show what is in the heart of such an eccentric, such a nobody.

This is my ambition, which is based less on resentment than love in spite of everything, based more on a feeling of serenity than on passion.

—The Hague, on or about July 21, 1882

In drawings such as "Sorrow" he had succeeded in expressing on paper what he saw not only with the eye of an artist but also with the heart of a compassionate man.

IN IT WITH HIS HEART

Every week I make one thing or another that I could not make before, and that is what I meant, it is like growing young again. And the awareness that nothing (except illness) can take the power away from me that is now

> *beginning to develop; it is this awareness that gives me courage for the future and helps me bear the many difficulties of the present. It is a wonderful thing to be able to look at something and find it beautiful, to think about it and to hold it fast, and then to say: I will draw that and work at it until it is done.*
>
> —The Hague, on or about April 6, 1882

Despite the force he felt within him, Vincent was experiencing personal troubles. The problem of sharing a household with Sien was compounded by the fact that his artist friends in The Hague had begun to shun him. Like his family, they too, looked unfavorably on his relationship with a prostitute. His cousin Mauve even went so far as to berate Vincent for living irresponsibly and accused him of unrightfully calling himself an artist:

> *Mauve blames me for having said, I am an artist. I will not take it back because it is self-evident that those words imply the meaning of "always seeking without ever perfectly finding." It is exactly the opposite of saying, "I already know it, I have already found it." As far as I know, those words mean "I seek, I hunt for it, I am in it with my heart."*
>
> —The Hague, on or about May 7, 1882

Mauve and the others cruelly mocked Vincent's mannerism; they criticized his appearance and found the source for his models deplorable. Here, too, Vincent defended himself:

> *To rummage in shipyards and in alleys and streets and inside houses, waiting rooms, even in pubs, that is not a pleasant job, except for an artist. As such, one would rather be in the dirtiest neighborhoods if there is something to draw rather than at a tea party with nice ladies. Unless one wants to draw ladies—then even for an artist a tea party is nice.*

I just want to say that searching for subjects, moving among working people, looking for and having troubles with models, drawing from nature on the very spot, is rough work, even at times dirty work. . . .

I, who did not feel at ease in a reasonably good coat in a fine store, who would not feel so now, and would certainly be tedious and boring, I am a very different person when I am at work somewhere on the Geest or on the heath or in the dunes. Then my ugly face and shabby coat fits perfectly in with the surroundings and I am myself and work with pleasure. . . .

I wish they could just accept me as I am. I draw not to annoy people, but to amuse them or to make them aware of things which are worth looking at and which not everybody knows about.

—The Hague, on or about April 23, 1882

Refreshingly unselfconscious in his letters to Theo, Vincent again referred to the illustrators for *The Graphic* who he admired and sought to emulate. They too found their models among the poor and downtrodden.

Do I lower myself by living with the people I draw, do I lower myself when I go into the houses of laborers and poor people, or receive them in my studio? It seems to me that my profession requires that, and only those who do not understand anything about painting or drawing would object to it.

—The Hague, on or about April 23, 1882

It is a fact that I often find myself in great misery, yet there is within me a calm, pure harmony and music. In the poorest little hut, in the dirtiest corner I see paintings and drawings. And as if through an irresistible urge, my mind is drawn toward them. More and more things get

> *left out, and the more they're excluded, the faster my eye is drawn to the picturesque. Art asks for persistent work, and work in spite of everything, and always through continuous observation.*
>
> —The Hague, on or about July 21, 1882

His former employer at the Goupil galleries joined the rest in rebuking Vincent, telling him that he had failed before and would fail again, this time as an artist, for his art was unsalable and without charm. But Vincent was convinced that he was on the right path. And he knew that he would always be viewed as different because of his conception of things and the subjects he wanted to draw. However, it caused him suffering to be rejected again, especially by those from whom he had hoped for encouragement. Acknowledging his difficult temperament, he asked Theo to speak to them and beg their forgiveness if he had done anything to hurt them:

> *Do not imagine that I think myself perfect or that I believe that it is no fault of mine that many people take me for a disagreeable character. I am often terribly and annoyingly melancholy, irritable, yearning as if hungering and thirsting, as it were, for sympathy; and when I do not get it, I become indifferent, have a cutting edge, and often even pour oil on the fire. I do not enjoy being in company, and dealing with people, speaking with them, is often painful and difficult. But do you know where quite a lot of this, though not everything, originates? Simply because of nervousness. I who am terribly sensitive, physically as well as morally, became this way only during those years when I was deeply miserable. Ask any doctor, and he will understand at once that those nights spent in the cold street or in the open, the anxiety to get bread, a constant stress because I had no work, the estrangement from friends and family, caused at least*

three-fourths of my peculiarities of temperament. Could not my disagreeable moods or times of depression be attributed to all this?

But you, or anyone who will take the trouble to think it over, will, I hope, not condemn me because of it, nor find me unbearable. I try to fight it off, but that does not change my temperament; and even though because of this I have a bad side, damn it, I do have a good side, too, and can't they take that into account also?

—The Hague, July 6, 1882

In many of his letters from The Hague Vincent grappled with misunderstandings and strained relationships. As always, writing helped him remain on course, solidifying his resolve to listen to the force within, driving him to draw with meaning and purpose. And after all, he reasoned with himself, it was to nature and not people that he should look for inspiration and encouragement:

I have had very little dialogues with other painters lately. I have felt none the worse for it. It is not the language of painters so much as the language of nature that one should listen to. I can now understand better than I did six months ago why Mauve said, "Just do not talk to me about Dupré [the French artist Julien Dupré], *but rather talk about the bank of that ditch," or something like that. That sounds crude and yet it is perfectly correct. The feeling for the things themselves, for reality, is of more importance than a feeling for pictures—at least, it is productive and more enlivening.*

Because I now have such a broad, such a comprehensive feeling for art and for life itself, of which art is the essence, it sounds so shrill and so contrived to me when people like Tersteeg [manager of the The Hague branch of Goupil] *try to hold me down.*

—The Hague, on or about July 21, 1882

Here, once again, Vincent was strengthening his own conviction to remain *in it with all his heart*, repeating:

> [Everyone] *who works with love and intelligence finds precisely in the very sincerity of his love for nature and art a kind of armor against the opinion of other people.*
>
> *Nature is also severe and, so to speak, hard, but never deceives and always helps us forward. So I do not count my falling into disgrace with Tersteeg or anyone else a misfortune, however much I regret it. That itself cannot be the real cause of misfortune. If I had no love for nature or my work, then I would indeed be unhappy. But the less I get along with people, the more I learn to trust nature and to concentrate on her.*
>
> —The Hague, July 26, 1882

6

Drenthe: Into the Wilderness

I am not afraid to face the future as long as I need not be involved in those things that I feel to be dishonest.

—The Hague, May 16, 1882

ALONE AGAIN

Theo continued to implore Vincent to leave Sien. Many letters went back and forth between the two brothers on this subject. Vincent's need for a model, his desire to have a family of his own, and his passionate belief of doing what was right made him stubbornly adhere to his desire to save her life and that of her two children.

> *I do not want her to sink back into that terrible state of illness and misery in which I found her and from which she is saved for the time being. This I undertook, this I must continue. I do not want her to ever feel deserted and alone again; I want her to know and to see in every way that I feel a tender love for her and hold the children in my heart.*
>
> —The Hague, July 19, 1882

Vincent thought about leaving The Hague and taking Sien and the children away from the friendless environment of The Hague, where Sien's family was constantly enticing her to return to prostitution—she would make more money that way. Vincent thought of going to the remote area of Drenthe in North Holland. But after living with Sien for more than a year, Vincent finally realized that she could not withstand the pull of her previous life. In reality, Vincent couldn't save Sien, and he could not be both an artist and a constant caretaker. He described the torment this caused.

> *If you could know precisely what goes on inside of me, and how, so to speak, I have spent part of myself on the woman, namely, forgetting every other thing and concentrating on getting her back on her feet; if you could empathize with my melancholy view of life which, however, does not make me indifferent to it; on the contrary, I prefer feeling my sorrow over this or that to forgetting it or becoming indifferent—if you could feel exactly how far I can find my serenity in worship of sorrow and not in illusion, then perhaps, even for you, brother, my inmost self would be very different and more detached from life than even you can imagine now. . . . Helping her has been a question of all or nothing from the very beginning. I could not give her money to live by herself sooner. I had to take her in with me if I wanted to do something that would be of any use to her. And in my opinion, the right way would have been to marry her and take her with me to Drenthe. But I admit that she herself, as well as the circumstances, didn't allow it. She is not kind, she is not good, but neither am I, and just the way we were, there was a serious attachment despite everything.*
>
> —The Hague, on or about September 6, 1883

"Despite everything," Vincent never did marry Sien and decided to leave for Drenthe without her. Vincent recounted for Theo how he made the break with Sien, that he talked with her about the need for him to leave because he couldn't afford to stay, in terms of finances and his own work. He told Sien that staying with her would lead to a failure in being able to sustain either of them. He asked her to separate—for a while or forever—but that they would remain friends. He asked her to stay as "straight" as possible. He quoted himself saying to Sien:

> *As long as I know that you will try doing your best and will not lose control of everything and that you remain good to the children, just as you know that I have been good to them—if only you behave so that the children always have a mother in you . . . then you will always remain good in my eyes.*
>
> —**The Hague, September 2, 1883**

Vincent said that Sien understood the reasons for going their separate ways, that she had her children to live for just as Vincent had to live for his art. Finally, with a heavy heart, for Vincent had become especially attached to the little baby boy, he gave up his studio on the Schenkweg. With his departure from The Hague, he abandoned the only semblance of a family life he would ever know. Pulling up his roots, he became once again a "stranger on the earth." Theo had forbidden him to go to their parents' home because he worried that Vincent would become too stressful a burden for them, causing another unhealthy upheaval in their lives. Vincent had therefore found the alternative destination of Drenthe. Remembering that other artists, one of them being the admired landscape painter Charles Daubigny, had spent time in isolation and had found inspiration in that remote part of the country, Vincent headed north, to the peat country of northern Holland.

DARK AND DREARY DAYS

> *Will things worsen or improve over time? I know nothing about that, but that I feel a terrible misery that cannot be shaken off. "In every life some rain must fall / And days be dark and dreary"* [quote from Longfellow] *that is true,*

> *it cannot be different, but I wonder if the number of dark and dreary days cannot sometimes become too large?*
>
> —Drenthe, on or about September 26, 1883

Vincent left The Hague, full of remorse and suffering from ill health and physical and emotional exhaustion. Drenthe became another Borinage of isolation from family and friends. However, surrounded once again by nature, he felt his spirits revive. He could walk through the fields—the peat fields of Drenthe—with the wide horizon circling around him:

> [I could] *find something to paint everywhere. It is exceedingly beautiful here, and I think that by painting I will learn to do it somewhat better. Now, my heart is in it, you do know that well. I also believe, moreover, that knowing a handicraft after all, that handicraft is the most solid means of existence, one reason more for me to keep seeking it there.*
>
> —Drenthe, on or about October 22, 1883

He had more time to write and spent his evenings reflecting on his life and capturing everything he saw in long letters to Theo. He wrote himself out of his misery, all the while also imparting encouraging messages to Theo:

> *Our aim, first and foremost, is to reform ourselves through craft and interaction with nature, believing that it is our duty first and foremost, precisely in order to remain straightforward with other people, and consistent.*
>
> *Our aim is "walking with God" in contrast to living amid the affairs of the big cities. Thereby we will do no one any harm.*
>
> *Our belief is that, yes—although to some people's understanding it may seem hypocritical to say this—our belief, I say, is that God helps those who help themselves in so*

> *far that they aim their efforts and attention on that and take their hands out of their sleeves to that end.*
>
> —Drenthe, on or about October 31, 1883

Vincent had always been convinced that *in order to grow, one must be rooted in the soil.* Back in the countryside, the lowly dark huts that dotted the peat fields flooded him with memories of the Brabant landscape. Being surrounded by a familiar world gave Vincent willpower and inspiration. He relished the dignity of the laborers. He was "at home," once again observing the peasants toiling hard, cutting their peat and loading it onto the low-lying barges that were pulled along the many canals. He made drawings and paintings of these peat diggers down in their ditches, where the women's white caps and the blue peasant smocks of the men contrasted with the rich dark browns of the soil. Some of his paintings seem to have been painted with the very pigments of the earth to convey the *dark and dreary* atmosphere of the landscape. The sketches of twisted roots and tree stumps sticking out of muddy clumps of wet grass expressed a melancholy that matched his moods. He felt nature commiserating with him, inviting him to accept her fecundity and healing power in the silence of the marshes. Nature revealed her serenity to a man who knew how to listen with his soul. So he responded to the inherent beauty in all the subdued tones of peat and heath. He painted what he heard and observed: the silhouettes of gnarled trees and peat-covered huts, water ditches reflecting the muted colors of the sky, and stooped-over peasants toiling along the canals. Daily he went further and further into the peat fields feeling the "marvelous scenes":

> *The longer I stay here the more beautiful I find it, and from the outset I will endeavor to stay in this region. For it's so beautiful here that a great deal of study is needed to make something of it, and only elaborate work can give a truer understanding of things as they fundamentally are, in order to express their serious, sober nature.*

> *I came across superb figures. But again, a nature that has so much nobility, so much dignity, and gravity, must be dealt with maturity and patience and long-drawn-out work.*
>
> —Drenthe, September 24, 1883

Alone in this wilderness, with no one and nothing to distract him, he could gain the maturity and patience needed to capture and internalize nature's "nobility, dignity and gravity."

SOMETHING DEEPER AND BETTER

> *In my opinion I am often very rich—not in money, but rich (though it doesn't happen every day) for the reason that I have found my work—something to which I can dedicate myself with all my heart and soul, and which inspires me and makes life meaningful.*
>
> *My moods change of course, but the average sentiment is serenity. I have a firm faith in art, a firm confidence in it being a powerful stream that—though he himself must do his bit, too—carries a man to harbor.*
>
> *At all events, I consider it such a great blessing when a man has found his work that I cannot count myself among the unhappy ones. I mean, I may have surely been in relatively great difficulties, and there were gloomy days in my life, but I would not want to be counted among the unlucky, nor would it be justified if I were.*
>
> —The Hague, March 11, 1883

The time in Drenthe served to solidify his calling to become an artist who was to live solely for his art. The fervent desire to serve and minister that had led him to the "people living in darkness" in the Borinage was now being transformed into "the powerful stream" of creating an art infused with spirit and humanity.

During the next three months Vincent tried to convince his brother to become an artist, too. This was partly due to his yearning for companionship as well as the knowledge that Theo was unhappy in his position at the Goupil establishment. And so Vincent began to daydream about the two of them living and painting together. By urging Theo to follow his heart's desire, to leave everything else behind, and to become an artist, Vincent's writing became obviously self-referential. His letters to Theo, especially at this time, were truly letters to himself:

> *What I think is the best life, oh without even the slightest doubt, is a life that consists of long years of being outside dealing with nature—and of the something on high which is unfathomable, "awfully Unnamable," because one cannot find a name for what is above that nature. Be a peasant; be, if at the present time that were appropriate, a village clergyman or schoolmaster; be, and given the present, this is the form that seems to me to fit the circumstances best, be a Painter—and as a person you will, after a number of years of outdoor life and manual work, as a person you will, by doing this, become something better and deeper in the end and in the passage of years. I believe this strongly. . . . If one starts, one must only do it with the belief in the need to be in contact with nature, with the belief that if one walks on that path one cannot come out wrong, and walks straightest. And added to that is just precisely that if things were easy, like living off some income, it would be of very little help, for it is precisely many a hard day, precisely many efforts done in vain, that make someone better.*
>
> —Drenthe, November 5, 1883

While unable to induce his brother to join him, Vincent nevertheless convinced himself to embrace fully the life of an artist. Once again in a desolate place, and in nature, he fulfilled the aspiration that had begun in the miner's hut in Cuesmes. Now in Drenthe, he took the final step of wholeheartedly accepting what was *best in life* for him in order to become *something better and deeper*. He would no longer be aiming to help, or teach, or save someone in need. This was the beginning of a life solely devoted to art, an art that would be founded in nature, and, for the time being, among the poor. He would now let his art language be the sole expression of his faith and compassion. All this would demand the sacrifice of his personal desires, including the aspiration for a family of his own. What he had read years earlier by Ernest Renan in *The Life of Christ* was to be the underlying motive for the path he now chose:

> *To act in this world one must die to oneself. . . . Man is not down here on earth merely to be happy, he is not even placed here to be simply honest. He is here to realize great things for humanity.*
>
> —London, May 8, 1875

For the remaining years of Vincent's life, his belief in "Something on High" and his art were fused into the supreme goal, his mission, to do great things for a suffering humanity through art:

> *And now, I say as brother to brother, as friend to friend, let us seek from now on, despite our austere youth and having gone against the grain, the gentle light, for which I know no other name but the white ray or goodness.*
>
> —Drenthe, on or about November 5, 1883

7

Nuenen: Peasant Painter

Besides, I desire nothing else than to live deep, deep in the heart of farming country and to paint peasant life. I feel that I can create my working environment there, and so I shall calmly keep my hand to the plough and cut my furrows.

—Nuenen, April 6, 1885

Painting rural life is a thing that will remain good. . . . It is no bad idea that in France town halls are being decorated with scenes from rural life. . . . But what would be better is that the pictures of peasants are displayed in houses, in illustrations and other reproductions, directly among the people.

—Nuenen, June 15, 1885

Despite Theo's admonition that he not return home, Vincent packed up his paints and brushes and headed to Nuenen, to the new parish in the Brabant where his parents were now living. Confronting his parents once again wasn't easy. He arrived on their doorstep in Nuenen carrying a large bag and some dark sketches and paintings, his only accomplishments since their last meeting. He was aware of their mistrust. He knew they feared his eccentric behavior and worried about the impact he might have on their reputation within the new parish. Their fears were justified. The sight of Vincent walking around town with his easel on his back, drew suspicious glances from his father's parishioners. But Vincent was at peace with his determination to become an artist of rural life:

> *When I say that I'm a peasant painter, it is truly so, and it will become more obvious to you in the future that I feel at home there. And it has not been in vain, that I've spent so many evenings sitting with the miners and the peat cutters and the weavers and peasants in their homes pondering by the fire, unless I was working too hard and had no time to think. Because I'm continually observing peasant life at all hours of the day, I'm so absorbed by it that I really hardly think of anything else.*
>
> —Nuenen, April 13, 1885

Vincent felt invigorated by the ability to work outdoors every day, by having a studio of sorts in the parsonage's "mangle room" (wash room) and by the abundance of subjects to draw everywhere. Painting peasant life gave him *peace of mind,* a certain serenity and a "home," despite *a lot of scrambling around and misery on the outside of life* (Nuenen, on or about June 22, 1885).

WRESTLING WITH NATURE

> *I see no other way than to work with the model. Of course one must not extinguish one's power of imagination, but it is precisely through looking continually at nature and wrestling with it, that the power of imagination is sharpened and made more truthful.*
>
> —The Hague, October 15, 1882

Vincent was back again in the countryside of his youth, surrounded by ploughed fields and small farms, by herds of sheep and peasants sowing, harvesting, and gleaning. He walked the country lanes and relentlessly sketched the scenes unfolding before his eyes, ordinary subjects that were *at the same time so beautiful that it is indeed worthwhile to devote one's life to expressing the poetry hidden in them* (The Hague, August 26, 1882).

While no longer consoling and comforting the poor, he was wholly absorbed in drawing them, spending time in the fields with them in their gardens and in their huts. Just as he had in Etten, he drew them as they were, in their soiled clothes, performing their everyday tasks. Vincent took part in the rhythms of sowing and harvesting, capturing the daily sights of the present to make them available in perpetuity. Continuing to be inspired by Millet and his peasant paintings, and by the fact that creating an honest, straightforward sentiment in his paintings was an ongoing battle—a "wrestling"—with the subjects before him, Vincent was persuaded that *those people do* not *get there who don't make wrestling with nature their essential concern:*

> *I think that if one has tried to follow the masters attentively, one will find them all at certain moments, deep in reality. What I mean is, what one calls their creations, one will also see in reality with similar eyes, with a similar sentiment as they had.*
>
> *In any case, whether people like or don't like what I do and how I do it, I, for my part, don't know any other way than to wrestle so long with nature until she reveals her secret to me.*
>
> —Nuenen, on or about January 26, 1885

And deep in the reality of rural life, Vincent sought to discover nature's secret within all that surrounded him. He was convinced that the tangible scenes of everyday temporal life pointed to a reality that existed beyond them. "What does not pass" was revealed "in what passes" (Nuenen, on or about January 26, 1885). The infinite was manifested in the finite. In The Hague he had alluded to this when he wrote:

> *One of the things that will not pass is the something on high and belief in God, even if the forms change, a change that is as necessary as the renewal of greenery in the spring.*
>
> —The Hague, between December 13 and 18, 1882

From Nuenen he wrote about this again:

> *Isn't it a pity that you, for instance, seldom or hardly ever anymore go into those cottages, or relate to those people, or see those moods in the landscape, which were painted in the paintings you found to be the finest? I do not say that you can do this in your position, just because one must look much and long at nature before reaching the conviction that the most poignant things the great masters have painted are grounded in life and reality itself. A basis of sound poetry, which exists eternally as a fact, and can be found if one digs and seeks deeply enough. "Ce qui ne passe pas dans ce qui passe"* [what does not pass in what does pass], *it exists.*
>
> —Nuenen, on or about January 26, 1885

He wanted his art to sort out the mystery inherent in the natural world in order to make it intelligible for everyone to see. Vincent believed that what one could truly see and feel, one could also care for and love. It became his duty to make art that would draw people into a more intimate relationship with life. He created icons and emblems out of ordinary, everyday moments and human actions so that people could begin to "read" his art, be touched by it, and understand. He believed that art could be the vehicle through which the essence—the holiness—of the commonplace spoke, thereby allowing viewers to enter into the experience of the mystical, the "Something on High." Vincent once compared the scene in a Nativity painting, one in which he had found the true sentiment of the miraculous lacking, with a real birth in a stable. He had witnessed such a birth, the commonplace birth of a calf.

> *There was a little girl there, in that stable that night—in the Borinage—a little brown peasant face with a little white nightcap. She had tears in her eyes out of compassion for the poor cow when the poor animal was in the throes of labor and was having great trouble. It was pure, holy, wonderfully apparent, like a Correggio, a Millet, an Israëls.*
>
> —The Hague, March 11, 1882

The birth of a calf in a stable, likened to the birth of *the* Child in the stable of the Nativity, ordinary happenings in the stark reality of life pointing to something beyond, something holy. For Vincent such moments were always sources for art; art that in turn could point back to ordinary reality.

THE WEAVERS

> *The other one, with a dreamy air, almost pensive, almost a sleepwalker, that is the weaver.*
>
> —Cuesmes, September 24, 1880

> *For I believe that, after all, I have done nothing or shall never do, what would have had me lose or make me lose the right to feel myself a human being among human beings. . . . For my part, I often find it more pleasant to be among people who do not even know the word in question, for instance the peasants, the weavers, etc., than being in the more civilized world.*
>
> —Nuenen, on or about January 4, 1884

Weavers had intrigued Vincent ever since his days in Etten, when he had read the story about a weaver in George Eliot's novel

Silas Marner. He had also written about walking through weavers' villages on a long excursion while living in the Borinage:

> *Another thing that I saw during this excursion were the weavers' villages. The miners and the weavers are somewhat of a race apart from other workmen and artisans and I have a great sympathy for them and would count myself happy if one day I could draw them, so that these unpublished or as yet almost unpublished types, could be brought into greater awareness. The man from the bottom of the abyss, "de profundis," that is the miner; the other one . . . is the weaver. It is now almost two years already that I am living with them and have, to some extent, come to know their unique character, at least mainly that of the miners. And more and more I find something touching and so heartrending even in these poor and little-known workers, the lowest of all, so to speak, and the most despised, which one usually thinks about, thanks perhaps to the effect of a vivid, but very false and unjust, imagination, as a race of criminals and robbers.*
>
> —Cuesmes, September 24, 1880

Many of the laborers in and around Nuenen were also weavers, another people set apart, like the miners in the Borinage, a "disinherited race." His parents thought them to be peddlers, grinders, and rootless men of unconventional habits. But despite his parents' attitude, and at the same time intensifying their sense of disapproval, Vincent sought closer contact with the weavers, spending countless hours inside their lowly, cramped huts. He squeezed himself beside their large looms and sketched them, following the desire he had expressed years before.

He created a whole series of dark drawings and paintings of weavers imprisoned inside the square-rigged structure of their giant looms. With each successive image of a weaver he hoped to uncover and paint their peculiar character. He tried to convey what it was like to do nothing all day long but send the shuttle to and fro through the weft. In some of his drawings, the weavers sit beside a window that leads the eyes from the dark interior to warm sunlit gardens outside—a tantalizing freedom that lay just beyond their reach, for they were trapped beside their looms to earn their daily bread. Vincent managed to recreate the atmosphere of despondency, drudgery, and sacrifice. What reactions would viewers have to such images? Empathy? Indifference? Would they look at their own clothes and realize they originated within the dismal confines of the weavers' huts? Would such a realization elicit gratitude and recognition of the sacrificial labor of another human being? Vincent could certainly identify with the weavers' experience of being caged in. He too felt imprisoned by his own poverty, by not being able to live without the support of Theo, by his obsessive drive to do nothing but draw. But it was a prison he imposed on himself for he had no desire to do anything apart from his vocation. And just like the weavers who wouldn't abandon their looms, he too would remain attached to his brushes, his easel, and his reed pens, fulfilling his duty to create art that would benefit humankind. He too lost himself in the present moment, like the weavers tirelessly at work:

> *That blending oneself with the present moment, that being so completely carried away and inspired by the surroundings in which one happens to be, what can one do about it? And even if one wanted to resist it, how useful would that be? Why shouldn't one give in to that which is right there, for this, after all, is the surest way to be able to create something.*
>
> —Nuenen, between February 18 and 23, 1884

The weaver paintings became narratives of a soon to be lost handiwork. They memorialized the skilled craft of laborers who were being replaced by the more profitable machines of the industrial era.

THE POTATO EATERS

> *I don't yet know beforehand what I shall do with those heads, but I want to obtain the motif directly from their personality.*
>
> —Nuenen, December 30, 1884

Vincent had worked at drawing genre images while in The Hague to show groups of people in different settings, such as people lining up at the soup kitchen. In Nuenen, he began to plan a painting involving several members of a family of peasants. He was an admirer of Jozef Israëls's work and called him the "Dutch Millet," especially for his paintings of peasant families sharing a meal, such as "A Frugal Meal," or "A Peasant Family at the Table." Observing a family of potato farmers hard at work in their fields and visiting them in their dark huts, Vincent thought of showing them gathered together for their evening meal. For him it was more than a family sitting around a table:

> *These people, who by the light of their little lamp are eating their potatoes, who with the same hands that are reaching into the dish have tilled the earth, and so this painting speaks of manual labor and thus of having honestly earned their food.*
>
> —Nuenen, April 30, 1885

This painting was to be about connecting the hardships of the peasants' labor to the sustenance—the nourishment—they needed for survival and for the strength to keep on laboring; it was to be about the essence of their fate of constant toil. The painting had to tell the story of the kinship and shared struggle of an ordinary peasant family. This was also going to be a painting that expressed Vincent's values, his focus, and his priorities: a family united by their shared lot in life, coming together for a time of communion, the sacred moment of a common meal. By representing the harsh reality of the peasantry not as a romanticized view of rural life but in all truthfulness, Vincent planned on creating a truly modern painting. His parents and even Theo didn't see much in this plan.

After countless portrait studies and hours spent with the De Groot family, Vincent memorialized them in his painting "The Potato Eaters." It is a dark and gloomy painting where even the light of the lamp hanging above the table is muted and almost overcome by the somber interior of the cabin. Vincent admitted that it was not a beautiful image, that it was coarse and smelled of smoke and freshly dug earth, and that the colors were those of a very dusty potato, *unpeeled of course* (Nuenen, on or about May 2, 1885). According to Vincent, it would benefit city folk to experience a bit of rural life, even in the form of a painting. He also felt that art did not have to be beautiful in order to be good; what was important was that it be authentic, portraying in all honesty a real situation, "giving form and strength to his thought and inspiration" (The Hague, November 5, 1882):

> *At the point where I now am, however, I see the chance of rendering the feeling of the impression I have of what I see. Not always literally precise—rather never precise—for one sees nature through one's own disposition.*
>
> —Nuenen, April 9, 1885

> *What I am trying to get at is not that I can draw a hand but the gesture, not a head with mathematical precision, but the overall expression. . . . In a word: life.*
>
> —Nuenen, on or about May 22, 1885

Vincent never considered the aim of art to render everything academically correct and perfect. He had no patience for artists who painted with *cool heads, who think themselves "above such things." Instinct, inspiration, impulse, conscience, these guide one more honestly than many people think* (Nuenen, on or about June 2, 1885). Vincent felt that these were precisely the things that created good art, for true artists were guided by their sentiments, their soul. The paintings of the salon artists were rendered faultlessly, according to proper technique, but lacked passion:

> *Do you know in the old Dutch school a single digger, a single sower??? Did they ever seek to paint "a laborer"? . . . Working, that is what the figures in the old paintings are not doing . . . I should be desperate if my figures were good, . . . I do not want them to be academically correct, . . . If one photographs a digger, he certainly would not be digging then . . . in my eyes, Millet and Lhermitte are the true artists, because they do not paint things as they are, examined in a dry analytical way, but as they—Millet, Lhermitte, Michelangelo—feel them.*
>
> —Nuenen, on or about July 14, 1885

The note from Vincent that accompanied "The Potato Eaters" canvas sent to Theo in Paris read, *There is some passion in what I am sending you* (Nuenen, May 4 and 5, 1885). The peasants on Vincent's canvases became the "heroes" of his painted stories. Their verisimilitude was the evidence that their story was based on real life:

> *Peasant life is something serious, and I, for one, would blame myself if I didn't try to make paintings that would give serious things to think about to people who think seriously about art and about life. . . . One must paint the peasants as being himself one of them, as feeling, thinking as they do themselves.*
>
> —Nuenen, April 30, 1885

Viewers standing before "The Potato Eaters" had to come to understand intuitively that the existence and purpose of these ordinary peasants sitting down for a meal was intricately tied to their own. These peasants were sharing what they had grown and harvested with a much larger table beyond the confines of their hut. Vincent had to strengthen the expressive quality of his subjects in order to more forcefully have this reality affect all those who would gather around the table of these potato eaters in the future. He had to exaggerate their haggard and worn-out features. Even though Vincent had studied the peasants and the interior of their hut during hours of observation, he told a deliberate lie in his portrayal of them, in the hope of communicating the circumstances of their sacrificial toil more compellingly (Nuenen, on or about October 10, 1885):

> *My great desire is to learn to make such inaccuracies, such deviations, reworkings, changes of what is there in reality, so that they may become, well yes, lies if one likes, but truer than the literal truth.*
>
> —Nuenen, on or about July 14, 1885

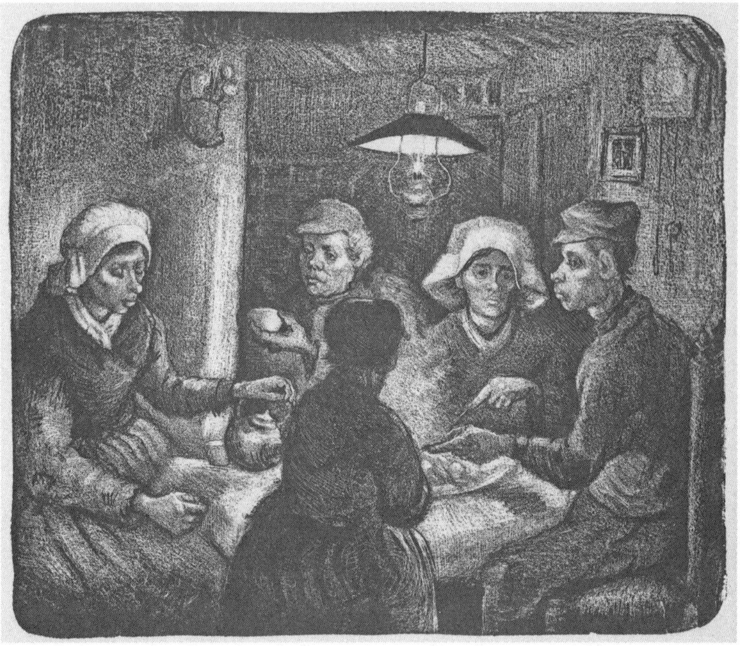

The Potato Eaters. Nuenen: April 1885. Used with permission of the Van Gogh Museum, Amsterdam (Vincent van Gogh Foundation).

With "The Potato Eaters" Vincent emulated the subject matter found in Jozef Israëls's paintings, but he achieved simultaneously the mysterious effect of a narrative image by Rembrandt who could express the deeper meaning of an ordinary moment or of a biblical story without any words. Vincent's "The Potato Eaters" and the weaver paintings were once again his attempt to depict in his "language" what Rembrandt, Israëls, Daumier, and Dickens, Hugo, Eliot, and Zola did in theirs.

STILL LIFE WITH BIBLE

> *I must tell you that painting does not seem so strange to me as you may think. On the contrary, I like it very much because it is a powerful means of expression. And at the same time one can say delicate things with it, too—a soft grey or green can speak in the midst of roughness.*
>
> —The Hague, August 10 and 11, 1882

While working hard at his drawing, first in the washroom-turned-studio of the parsonage, then in a rented room in the rectory, Vincent continued to have disagreements with his parents. Vincent and his father renewed their old arguments about his passion for the realist novels of his day, with Vincent trying unsuccessfully to convince his father that the Gospel message was as clearly expressed in contemporary novels as it was in the Bible. Vincent's rebellious arguments deeply affected and disturbed Pastor Van Gogh, who felt that his son berated his faith and life work. It affected the relationships within the whole family. Once again, the tense atmosphere in the parsonage became unbearable. Vincent desperately sought approval for his own convictions, but his argumentative and contemptuous attitude prevented any reconciliation. Father and son never had the chance to resolve their differences. Upon returning home from a pastoral call one day, Pastor Theodorus Van Gogh collapsed in the entrance of the parsonage and died soon thereafter.

The moment so movingly depicted in Ary Scheffer's image of a fatherly embrace in "The Prodigal Son," the print hanging in the pastor's study, never came to pass between Vincent and his father. This would haunt Vincent for the rest of his life. Writing to his mother in letters years later, he would seek forgiveness for having caused his father such grief.

Before leaving the parsonage after the death of his father, Vincent painted one of his most personally expressive paintings: "Still Life with Bible." The painting shows an old Bible (possibly his father's) resting on a table, opened to the passage of "The Suffering Servant" in the book of Isaiah. The letters identifying the Old Testament passage are visible in the top margin of the right page: ISAEI. A solitary tall candleholder with an extinguished candle stands next to the Bible. Below the Bible lies a very well-read and worn-out copy of the novel *La Joie de Vivre* (The Joy of Living) by Emile Zola. Zola's words from his introduction to this novel give a sense of the powerful story:

> *She* [Pauline Quenu, the servant girl] *would remain unmarried in order to be able to work for universal deliverance. And she was, indeed, the incarnation of renunciation, of love for others and kindly charity for erring humanity. She had stripped herself of everything, but happiness rang out in her clear laugh.*

Vincent felt that the people in some of his favorite Zola novels were truly human. He chose to juxtapose the novel about Pauline Quenu with the Isaiah passage in the Bible precisely because he felt that Emile Zola wrote a suffering servant story for a modern audience. Vincent in essence was visually displaying the issue of contention between his father and himself. His father did not accept substitutes for the biblical stories. In Vincent's view, finding the same type of stories in contemporary novels did not diminish the value of the Bible; on the contrary, it affirmed inherent truths. Biblical stories could speak through modern protagonists to an audience far removed from biblical times in the holy lands. While Vincent painted his father's Bible in heavy, lifeless grays and browns, he nevertheless subtly applied brush strokes of the complementary colors orange and blue on its pages. Barely visible, these colors vibrate on the open pages of the Bible, indicating that the Holy Word is still "alive" and relevant, yet just as vibrant as the story next to it with its warm, lively, yellow-hued cover.

In "Still Life with Bible" we see a change in Vincent's painting style. He had made a trip to Amsterdam to see the newly designed and recently opened building of the Rijksmuseum:

> *Yearning most of all for Rembrandt and Frans Hals, I'm going one day this week to the museum in Amsterdam with an acquaintance of mine. If I can make connections for my own work, I won't fail to do that, and I firmly believe if I persevere in that, I'll win. . . . I believe that surely my work will benefit in the long run if I see more paintings, because when I see a painting I can ascertain what was done with it.*
>
> —Nuenen, October 4, 1885

What he brought back from this visit was a new discovery of painting styles seen in paintings by Frans Hals: bold colors and spontaneity of painting that revealed the traces of individual brush strokes. On this visit, Vincent was also reminded of the artist Delacroix, of whom it was said, "*Lorsque Delacroix peint, c'est comme le lion qui devore le morceau*" [when Delacroix paints, it is like the lion devouring his piece (of meat)] (Nuenen, on or about October 13, 1885). From a reading of Delacroix's treatise on colors,Vincent had gleaned the insight that color had a powerful expressive quality and that the artist could use color suggestively and not solely as observed. These two techniques, the suggestive use of color and the "unfinished" spontaneity of visible brushstrokes, would in time become Vincent's hallmarks.

In the still life painting of the Bible (his first application of these new discoveries) he attempted to express his emotions following his father's death. By painting the still life spontaneously, *in one stroke—but with absolutely complete exertion of one's whole spirit and attention* (Nuenen, on or about November 7, 1885), and by using colors suggestively, Vincent interwove his personal feelings with a unique method of painting. He gave a visual voice to his sorrow, his regret, his longing for forgiveness, which, taken together, made for a powerful plea for spiritual reconciliation. The extinguished candle next to the Bible dramatizes death, but the subtle complementary colors blue and orange vibrating on the pages of the Bible reveal life. Thus Vincent succeeded in blending the holy and timeless scriptures of the Bible into the meaning of life, personal loss, and eternal truths that connected the present with the past and future. The painting is a masterwork, a tribute finally to a father he had loved, who had years before introduced him to the Bible and the story of Jesus around the dining table in the Zundert parsonage. Vincent chose Isaiah, chapter 53, because it summed up the understanding of Jesus with which he so strongly identified. Vincent too was a man of sorrows acquainted with grief, despised and rejected.

The Van Gogh family home dissolved after the death of Pastor Van Gogh. His mother's mistrust of her son's occupation made the fracture complete:

> *Only it is certain that Ma is utterly unable to comprehend that painting is a faith, and that it implies the duty to not be disturbed by public opinion, and that it is through perseverance that one wins and not by giving in, and "Faith I cannot give thee" is exactly the case between her and me, as it was with Pa and remained so.*
> —Nuenen, April 6, 1885

There would no longer be a parsonage to return to as a place of refuge. There would be no earthly father waiting for his prodigal son. Vincent left Nuenen, never again to set foot in his native country.

Part III

Life and Art Are One

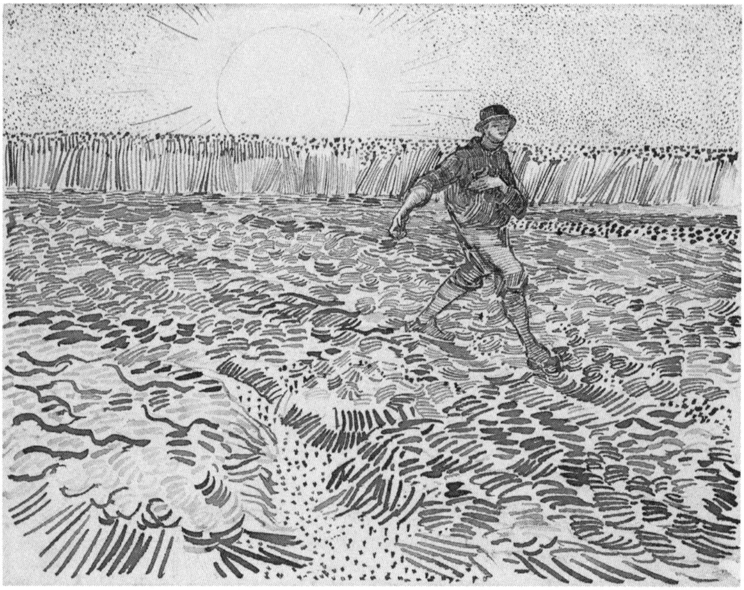

The Sower. Arles: August 6-8, 1888. Used with permission of the Van Gogh Museum, Amsterdam (Vincent van Gogh Foundation).

8

Paris: The Artist's Voice

> *I imagine more and more, however, that art for art's sake, working for the sake of working, energy for energy's sake, is after all the principle of all great men. . . . But in painting one finds a certain rest in the histories of those painters who aimed at the most sublime despite it all.*
>
> *Israëls himself, for instance, was still quite unknown and still poor, even to the extent of having nothing but dry bread to eat—when he nevertheless wanted to go to Paris, even though the circumstances were discouraging enough.*
>
> —Antwerp, on or about February 2, 1886

Theo and Vincent had spoken about living together in Paris. But on leaving home Vincent traveled first to Antwerp, hoping to connect with the artist community there. He enrolled in some classes at the academy. After reacting insubordinately at having to copy plaster casts rather than draw from live models he was chastised and demoted to the lowest classes. There he was forced to copy plaster models of ears and noses. For a man who had been sketching real people, such basics of an academic training were demeaning. For him the highest artistic aim was *to paint human beings, that was the old Italian art, that is what Millet did and what Breton does* (Antwerp, December 28, 1885). That is what Vincent needed to do: *I feel a true power in me because, wherever I may be, I'll always have a goal—painting people as I see them and know them* (Antwerp, between January 12 and 16, 1886). He had also spent years drawing out-of-doors and did not feel those were wasted, for *that is just the thing that those who haven't been anywhere else except in academies and studios lack—the ability to see the reality in which they live* (Antwerp, on or about February 4, 1886) and to find there the subjects to draw. He observed how the academy students drew; it was all *completely correct, it is whatever you like, but it is* dead (Antwerp, on or about February 11, 1886). Antwerp was not the place to improve his art. Without further delay he decided to leave for Paris to join Theo, who received short notice in a scribbled note:

> *Don't be angry with me that I've come all of a sudden. I have thought about it so much and I think like this we'll save time. Will be at the Louvre from midday on, or earlier if you like.*
>
> —Paris, on or about February 28, 1886

There was nothing else for Theo to do but welcome his brother into his life and into his apartment for the next two years. It became a turbulent and challenging time for both. Theo was at this time an art dealer of nineteenth-century Academy art at the Goupil establishment. His work was demanding, requiring that he be well rested and levelheaded, and look presentable. That became almost impossible, amid the chaos and upheaval that Vincent brought into his life. Vincent's passions ran high, he was unorganized, unkempt, and left a trail of disorder wherever he went, dropping paint tubes on the floor and often using Theo's socks or anything he could find to wipe his canvases. Moreover, he had the habit of marching into Theo's bedroom at any time of the night to engage in animated arguments about art, arguments no doubt carried over from impassioned debates in the Bohemian cafés along the boulevards.

For several centuries, the French Academy of Art had been determining the rules of what constituted a work of art. But in the early 1800s things began to change. Rather than fulfilling commissions by wealthy patrons, artists were beginning to use their canvases to express what *they* had to say. They rebelled against the institutional constraints imposed by the Academy, looking for subject matter relevant to them and to their times. Artists were creating bold new art manifestos and breaking all the rules. Art was becoming the voice of the artist. Vincent was already convinced that art was his language, and that whatever he painted or drew should express his temperament and contain his feelings:

> *Though Zola, in my opinion, makes colossal mistakes in his judgment of paintings, he says in* Mes Haines *a beautiful thing about art in general "Dans l'oeuvre d'art je cherche, j'aime l'artist"* [in the work of art I look for—I love—the artist].
>
> —Nuenen, on or about July 14, 1885

Soon after his arrival in Paris, Vincent painted his first of many self-portraits—poised at his easel with palette and brush in hand, clad in an artist's smock, felt hat on his head, painted in the somber Dutch colors of Rembrandt. He looked the true Parisian artist, dapper and self-confident, inspired by George Duroy, the main character in Guy de Maupassant's book *Bel Ami.* In the novel, Duroy eases his way into the high society of Paris thanks to his charm and congenial cheerfulness, qualities Vincent lacked. Still, he hoped that by at least trying to emulate Duroy's style he would find some inroads into the right social groups, gain acceptance and recognition, and at the same time make the acquaintance of female models willing to pose for him. Failing to find such models, he turned instead to flower arrangements and setting up his easel outdoors to paint Montmartre and city life. With loose brush strokes and the newly available synthetic pigments on his canvases, the subdued moods of the north gave way to the eclectic and electrically charged atmosphere of Paris.

THE COLOR OF LIGHT

> *What colors are in a painting, that surely is enthusiasm in life—therefore, it is no small matter to seek to preserve it.*
>
> —Antwerp, on or about January 2, 1886

The official Academy jurors banned paintings by the Impressionist artists from the Paris Salons, deeming their work unfinished and nontraditional. By the time Vincent arrived in Paris in May 1886, the Impressionists had begun organizing their own exhibitions. Rather than making faithful and studious imitations, many of the artists, using loose brushstrokes and dabs of color tried to capture the ephemeral quality of reflected light as it appeared to them in the present moment. Influenced by the landscape painters of the Barbizon School, who had forsaken their studios and fled into the bustling life outside to paint "en plein air," the Impressionists were to be found on the crowded boulevards, in the parks and forests, the cafés, laundry rooms, cabarets, and along the banks of the river Seine. They were painting "real life"—"the reality in which they lived." Vincent lost no time to join them:

> *If I now look into real life, I get the same kind of impression. I see the people in the street, well, but I often think the servant girls so much more interesting and beautiful than the ladies, the workmen more interesting than the gentlemen. And in those common girls and fellows I find a power and vitality, which if one wants to render them in their peculiar character, it ought to be done with a firm brush stroke, with a simple technique.*
>
> —Antwerp, December 14, 1885

The short, visible brush strokes of these *plein-air* artists became the *simple technique* with which Vincent continued to experiment, having already noticed this style of painting in the art of Frans Hals. But more than the "unfinished look" of the dabbed and stippled brush strokes, Vincent was fascinated by the way contrasting colors, loosely painted side by side, were combined by the eye of the viewer into an array of different vibrant hues. The scenes on the canvases of the Impressionists came to life with the luminous quality of light.

THE FLOATING WORLD

> *And one cannot study Japanese art, it seems to me, without becoming more cheerful and much happier and that makes us come back to nature, despite our education and our work in a conventional world.*
>
> —Arles, September 23 or 24, 1888

Since the early 1800s, the art market in Paris had become saturated with Japanese prints. The art of Japan had, in fact, been instrumental in making the Barbizon School artists look to nature for their inspiration and to the outdoors as their studio. Their subject matter highlighted what the Japanese artists found worthy to paint: scenes celebrating nature and the commonplace activities of daily life. The Japanese ukiyo-e woodblock prints reflected these fleeting moments—the "floating world"—and their influence was apparent in much of the art created in Paris during these years. Artists emulated the fluid bold lines and saturated colors, the unbalanced arrangement of subject matter, the unusual angles of perspective seen in Japanese art. These methods added a sense of movement and spontaneity to their work that was lacking in traditional compositions of Western art. The Japanese belief that a deep relationship with nature was the foundation for art resounded within Vincent. He became an enthusiastic admirer of all things Japanese and imagined the Japanese artist to be wise mentors:

> *If one studies Japanese art, then we see a man, undeniably wise and a philosopher and intelligent, who spends his time—doing what?—studying the distance from the earth to the moon?—no; studying Bismarck's politics?—no; he studies a single blade of grass.*
>
> *But this blade of grass leads him to draw all the plants, then the seasons, the great aspects of the landscapes, finally animals, and then the human figure. That is how he spends his life, and life is too short to do it all.*
>
> *Just think, isn't it almost a true religion that these simple Japanese teach us, and who live in nature as if they themselves were flowers?*
>
> —Arles, September 23 or 24, 1888

Already as a child Vincent had *studied a single blade of grass*, or a flower or observed intensely the peasants working the soil. In order to create meaningful paintings he had to love what he perceived, and this love came from having first seen an ordinary thing and discovering it to be extraordinary, a thing to be revered. He sensed this reverence in the art of the Japanese and looked to their style and methods to imbue his paintings with greater depth and vitality.

DISCOVERING MONTICELLI

> *Monticelli sometimes took a bouquet of flowers as his subject so that he could gather on a single panel the whole range of his richest and most perfectly balanced tones. One has to go straight to Delacroix to find such an orchestration of colors.*
>
> —Arles, on or about March 25, 1888

Not many letters exist from Vincent's time in Paris, but one can imagine the two brothers sharing their enthusiasm and vast knowledge of art and artists; the one they both came to admire greatly was Adolphe Monticelli.

Monticelli had lived in Paris for several years and had joined the painters of the Barbizon School in 1855 during the early years of *plein-air* painting. By 1870 he returned to his native Marseille where he continued to live solely for his art, while achieving little recognition. He died in poverty in 1886, the year Vincent arrived in Paris. Monticelli had developed a painting style of short dappled brush strokes with which he almost sculpted richly colored, viscous paint onto his canvases. This created a textured surface that reflected light, adding liveliness to his paintings by making the colors sparkle even more. When Monticelli was criticized for this rather unorthodox painting style, he remarked that he painted in this manner to be understood thirty years hence. Thirty years later Vincent and Theo stood in admiration and awe before Monticelli's work exhibited in Paris.

The painterly freedom Vincent had admired in Frans Hals' art was prevalent in the loose and visible brush strokes of his contemporaries in Paris. But now he discovered that Monticelli, a generation before, had already painted in this unique way, defying the art traditions of his time:

> *One sees that the greatest and most energetic people of the century have always worked against the grain and with them the work was always the result of their personal initiative. Both in painting and in literature (I'm not sure if this is the case with music, but I imagine it would have been the same). To begin something on a small scale, to persevere despite it all, to produce much with a small capital, to have character instead of money, more audacity than credit. Look at Millet and Balzac, Zola . . . Look at Delacroix.*
>
> —Antwerp, on or about January 29, 1886

Millet, Balzac, Zola, Delacroix—these were some of Vincent's standard bearers. Monticelli became one of them, too, especially when Vincent discovered that this artist had also been greatly influenced by Delacroix. Delacroix had emphasized that color was the first quality seen in a painting. Before form and content were distinguished, color had already affected the viewer on an unconscious level. Color, as the German poet Johann Wolfgang von Goethe had exclaimed, was the language of the soul. Delacroix and Monticelli were colorists who applied their color contrasts and vivid resonant tones intentionally and symbolically. Vincent, standing before their paintings, was emotionally affected by their work. His spirit quickened, just as it did whenever he watched the sun set in a rose-colored sky, or stood beside fields of golden wheat, or saw in the distance the glowing squares of lamplit cottage windows at dusk. Months before Vincent had written that Delacroix *makes us feel the life of things, and the expression, and the movement and that he has absolutely reached something* beyond the paint (Antwerp, December 14, 1885). Transitioning more and more from only drawing with reed pens and crayons to painting, Vincent had written from Nuenen that his palette was beginning "to thaw":

> *The barrenness of the earliest beginnings is gone. Often I still run into a blank wall when undertaking something, but all the same, the colors follow one another on their own, and taking one color as the starting-point I see clearly in my mind's eye what will be derived from it, and how one can get life into it. . . .*
>
> *Color Expresses Something in Itself. That one cannot miss; one must make use of it. What is beautiful, really beautiful—is also correct.*
>
> —Nuenen, on or about October 28, 1885

Vincent's paintings in Paris evolved from the thawing of his Dutch palette to the richly colored and textured paintings that have become his hallmark. He was experimenting with the luminous painting style of the Impressionists. He had become aware of the effects of color on the human psyche and was drawn into the expressive color dynamics found on Delacroix's and Monticelli's canvases. In painting he was learning not to just *make it as I see it,* but *to make it as I feel it* (The Hague, September 17 or 18, 1882), using his colors more suggestively and subjectively.

MOVING BEYOND IMPRESSIONISM

> *But the painter of the future will be a colorist like we have never had before. Manet prepared the ground, but you know well that already the Impressionists used a richer color than Manet. This painter of the future—I can't imagine him living in little cafés, working away with false teeth, and going to the Zouaves' brothels. . . .*
>
> *But it seems to me that I'm right when I feel that it will happen in a later generation, and that as far as we are concerned, we must work within our means toward that end, without doubting and without wavering.*
>
> —Arles, May 4, 1888

The art scene in Paris was in flux. Vincent could see the progression in the expressive nature of art since his early years in the art dealing business. He could also see the qualities in art that endured. *Certainly color is progressing* [mainly because] *of the Impressionists, even when they are going astray. But already Delacroix was more complete than they* (Arles, May 3, 1889).

Vincent's two-year stay in Paris was an emergent time for him but also for the new group of artists that had begun to develop yet another style and approach to art. These artists loosely called Symbolists believed that only eccentric social outsiders could pursue their true inner calling. They began moving away from the Impressionist subject matter that described the transitory moments of bourgeois life. They were hungering for an art that would go deeper than the sunlit surfaces of things. Their colors became more solid and static without the spontaneity and visibility of individual brush strokes. These artists looked to their imagination for form and content in their paintings, creating mythical scenes that would point to the deeper mysteries, the invisible and spiritual aspects of life. Vincent was intrigued by their approach to art and formed friendships with two of them, Emile Bernard and Paul Gauguin. Always eager to learn and explore, Vincent added their painting styles to his own experiments. But future letters between these friends reveal the fundamental differences in their philosophies and visions for art. Bernard and Gauguin trusted and relied on their imagination to assimilate the narrative elements in their paintings. For Vincent the story was already there, revealed in the natural world. It was the artist's task to "untangle" it and to make its metaphors and parables "intelligible to other people." Reality, nature, and the human figure as models, rather than imagination, always remained the basis for his art.

After two years of city life, Vincent longed for a calmer pace. Tired of being embroiled in polemics about the definition of art and painting methods, he was anxious to return to nature and devote all his time to painting. His stay in Paris had changed his painting style; it had loosened him up and added more light and greater emphasis on contrasting colors. But he was seeking something more substantial, more grounded, with more content, more Rembrandt and Millet:

> [I am returning more and more] *to what I was looking for before coming to Paris, and I don't know if anyone before me has spoken about suggestive color. But Delacroix and Monticelli, while not speaking about it, did it.*
>
> —Arles, September 18, 1888

His last self-portrait painted in Paris shows him surrounded by an Impressionist atmosphere of light, holding a palette of bright, saturated colors. He is, however, no longer a dapper looking

Parisian, but a "peintre ouvrier" (workman painter), wearing the blue smock of a peasant painter, longing to return to toil once again among the peasants working the fields. Packing his art tools and tubes of new vibrant paint, he turned his back on the Parisian life and boarded a train heading south. He would miss Theo, but the brothers both needed some distance to find each other again. This would happen, as always, through their letters.

Vincent intended to travel as far south as possible. Two motivating factors set his course. He had decided to go to Marseille to be closer to the town where Monticelli had lived and died. He was also searching for a place where a different light would intensify all colors, as seen on the ukiyo-e woodblock prints of the Japanese. From having admired Monticelli's Provence paintings, Vincent knew that he would find such colors in the South. At the same time he had the *pretentions of continuing the job that Monticelli started* (Arles, on or about November 21, 1888), hoping to achieve the essence of what this great artist, and all the serious masters, expressed in their work.

9

Arles: The Essence of Things

To get at the real character of things here, one must look at them and paint them for a long time.

—Arles, September 26, 1888

In February 1888, en route to Marseille, Vincent's train stopped in the station of Arles. He looked intently out the window. What met his gaze beyond the station made him jump up and spontaneously disembark. A late winter snow had recently dusted blooming fruit trees in an orchard bordering the train tracks. There were rows and rows of trees glistening in delicate colors under a pale winter sun. Marseille could wait.

After securing a room in a little hotel, Vincent set out to paint those orchards in bloom, trying out different painting styles: the feathery Impressionism of Monet and Renoir, the dashed marks of Signac and Pissarro, and Emile Bernard's cloisonné (dark outlined) shapes and flat colors. As the spring sun began to warm the orchards and melt the snow, everything began to dazzle with greater intensity. What he beheld all around him now were landscapes he recognized as true Monticellis:

Under the blue sky, the patches of orange, yellow, and red flowers achieve an amazing brightness, and in the limpid air there's something that's happier and more suggestive of love than in the North. It vibrates—like . . . a Monticelli.

—Arles, August 8, 1888

Monticelli hadn't imagined anything but had looked long and hard at the natural world of his native Provence; the vibrancy of colors under the heat of the sun could only be achieved by applying his unorthodox painting style—thick paint with a texture that reflected light:

> *I hadn't thought that when leaving Paris I would have found Monticelli and Delacroix so true. It's only now, after months and more months, that I am starting to distinguish that they didn't imagine anything. And I think that next year you'll see the same subjects of orchards, the harvest, again, but with a different color and above all with a changed technique. And that will continue, these changes and these variations.*
>
> —Arles, September 23 or 24, 1888

After painting nature in the Provence throughout a whole year Vincent wrote to Theo:

> *I have a few studies, among others, a mulberry tree, all yellow on rocky ground standing out against the blue of the sky; in this study I think that you will see that I have found the track of Monticelli.*
>
> —Saint-Remy, October 5, 1889

BLOOMING ORCHARDS: PERMANENCE IN THE IMPERMANENT

> *For the invisible things of him from the creation of the world* are clearly seen, *being understood by the things that are made, even his eternal power and Godhead.*
>
> —Romans 1:20

Vincent painted the orchards over and over again, hoping to distill onto his canvas the quality that attracted him so forcefully. Rather than the impressions of shimmering light reflecting off the surface of their leaves, he sought to capture the essence and the vitality permeating these blooming trees. Nature's message was there for all to see. Through the delicate impermanent blossoms crowning the tips of branches, nature manifested its permanence; the transitory blossoming of spring was part of an eternal cycle. The pink and white petals of the fruit trees were visibly revealing the invisible force of life. Once Vincent set up his easel among the orchards, he was completely, emotionally and physically, drawn into their splendor. With brush in hand he feverishly captured the gnarled tree trunks, the extending branches, and the explosion of blossoms. Vincent used his "shorthand" of lines, dabs, and colors to create icons for the celebration of springtime renewal. Nature was speaking through matter about spirit. He felt it. It was what the great masters had done: to let their painted subjects rise above nature and speak about a greater reality. He had already exclaimed in Nuenen that *it exists!* And from The Hague he had written that one could learn to *get a faith* by looking at a painting by Millet *where art is sometimes above nature.* In Millet's "Sower," he had observed, there *is more soul than in an ordinary sower in the field* (The Hague, January 3, 1883). To paint "more soul"—that was Vincent's ambition.

Besides the blooming trees, Vincent found other subjects that he painted and drew over and over, wholly absorbed—flowering gardens, clumps of grass, wheat fields, sunflowers. *It's looking at things for a long time that matures you and makes you understand more deeply* (Arles, September 23 or 24, 1888). This Zen-like practice of drawing the ten thousand ordinary things around him, until they were seen to be extraordinary miracles, remained a constant discipline for Vincent (Source: Frederik Frank, *The Zen of Seeing*). He looked long enough at what he drew until it became part of him, until he felt the subject:

> *Once I* feel *a motif*—know *it—then I* usually *make it in three or more variations, whether it's a figure or a landscape, but every time I involve nature for each one.*
>
> —Nuenen, on or about March 13, 1884

He consciously drew fast, not because he felt pressed for time to capture all that he saw, but because he believed, like the Japanese artists, that the drawings had to flow freely from what he perceived and sensed onto the paper through his pen:

> *I must warn you that everyone will think that I work too fast. Don't believe it. Is it not emotion, the sincere feeling for nature, that guides us, and—if the emotions are sometimes so strong that one works without realizing one works—when sometimes the strokes come with a flow and a coherence like words in a speech or a letter, then one must remember that it has not always been like this, and that in the future there will again be difficult days devoid of inspiration. Therefore one must strike while the iron is hot.*
>
> —Arles, on or about June 25, 1888

In Arles, Vincent's skills had progressed so far that, through the immediate interplay between the observed and the sketched, he could express his innate connection with the things of nature and translate onto paper what he "heard with his soul":

> *I consider that making studies is like sowing and that making paintings is like reaping. I believe one thinks more soundly when thoughts arise from direct contact with things, rather than when one looks at them with the intention of finding this or that in them.*
>
> —The Hague, September 18, 1882

Sketching quick studies, like meditating, was a way for Vincent to remain receptive to the compelling language of nature. When he painted (the "reaping"), he was under the strain of balancing the colors, of calculating their variations in tone and intensity in order to add the expressive depth of his emotions:

> *But you should know that I am in the midst of a complicated calculation, which results in a quick series of canvases quickly done but calculated long in advance. So now, when anyone says that they have been done too quickly, you can reply that they are the ones who have looked too quickly. . . . But during the harvest, my work was not any easier than that which the peasants who were harvesting were doing.*
>
> —Arles, on or about July 1, 1888

Vincent was in a frenzy of work, driven, relentlessly going after those orchards in bloom, or the olive trees, the cypresses, the wheat fields, the peasants at work, fully aware:

> *Not everyone would have the patience to let themselves be devoured by mosquitoes and to battle with the irritating annoyance of this constant mistral. Not to mention that I have spent days outside with a little bread and milk, since it was too far to return into town at any time.*
>
> —Arles, on or about July 13, 1888

He was in it with all his heart!

THE ETERNAL SOWER: A PARABLE IN PAINT

> *Flashes of memories of bygone days and a yearning for the infinite, of which the sower and the sheaf of corn are the symbols, still enchant me as before.*
>
> —Arles, on or about June 19, 1888

In the summer of 1888, Vincent created one of his most well-known paintings: "The Sower." On this canvas the familiar figure in the likeness of Millet's sower strides along the furrows of a freshly plowed field. He is strewing his seeds over clods of soil rendered in deep cool colors, with the reflections of light added in the warm complementary colors of orange and yellow. Against the horizon, in contrast to the still barren earth and spanning the width of the painting, stands a straight band of ripe golden stalks of wheat. The rays of a great yellow sun pulsate outward, filling the whole sky with a blaze of light. In the foreground, a path leading through the ploughed field and painted in a warm yellow-orange invites entrance into the painting:

> *Yesterday and today I worked on The Sower, which is done completely differently. The sky is yellow and green, the ground violet and orange. There is certainly a picture of this kind to be painted of this splendid subject, and I hope it will be done someday, either by me or by someone else.*
>
> *The question that remains is this.* "The Boat of Christ" *by Eugene Delacroix and Millet's* "The Sower" *are of an entirely different technique.* "The Boat of Christ" *(I speak of the sketch in blue and green with touches of violet, red and a little citron-yellow for the nimbus, the halo) speaks a symbolic language through color alone. Millet's sower is a colorless gray, the same as Israëls's pictures.*
>
> *Now, could one paint The Sower in color, with a simultaneous contrast of, for example, yellow and violet . . . yes or no? Why, yes, certainly. Well, do it then. Yes, that is also what old Martin says: "You must make the masterpiece." But go ahead and try it, and one falls into a whole metaphysics of color as is the case with a Monticelli, a mess from which it is damnably difficult to get out with honor.*
>
> *And it leaves one as absentminded as a sleepwalker. If only one could do something good. Well, let's remain*

> *full of courage and not despair. I hope to soon send you this attempt along with some others.*
>
> —Arles, on or about June 28, 1888

Vincent's "Sower" contains the whole cycle of life from birth to death and beyond, from an earthy fertility to the ripe harvest and radiant infinity. The figure of the sower stands firmly on the ground but reaches beyond the wheat, uniting both heaven and earth. "The Sower" contains a lively dialectic between the light of the sun and the darkness of the soil, between contrasting complementary colors, between the birth of germinating seeds and the harvesting of the ripe wheat. All these parts are woven together into an interpenetrating whole by Vincent's visible brush strokes. It is a tapestry of spring's receptive soil in blues and purples and summer's radiant yellow-oranges of a life-giving sun. Like Delacroix, Vincent's "Sower" speaks *a symbolic language through color alone*, colors that achieve the same vibrating quality subtly evident on the pages of the Nuenen still life of the Bible.

Vincent's thoughts and the painting of his nature "parables" were deeply rooted in Rembrandt, who had succeeded in making biblical stories come to life. Five months after painting this first sower, thinking *more about Rembrandt than may appear from my studies* he was working on *another sower. Immense citron-yellow disc for the sun. Green-yellow sky with pink clouds. The field is violet, the sower and the tree Prussian blue* (Arles, on or about November 21, 1888). In the choice of colors, Delacroix was very present, too, for this artist had *had a passion for the two colors, citron-yellow and Prussian blue* (Arles, on or about April 11, 1888). Apparent in the compositional design of Vincent's new version of "The Sower" is an element of a Japanese print with a dark tree trunk cutting diagonally across half of the painting and its large, flat areas of saturated paint. This sower is walking off the canvas toward the viewer, strewing seeds, engulfed in his own Prussian blue shadow. The flaming yellow disc of the sun radiates as a giant halo above his head. Here the figure of the sower rises above a commonplace laborer to the emblematic, symbolic giver of life, eternally sowing the seeds of renewal and hope.

Vincent would go on to create more agrarian parables and metaphors from the recognizable, ordinary things of the earth—fields of wheat, olive groves, laboring peasants, blooming flowers, starry skies—images that had multifaceted symbolic meanings throughout history and cultures. Two thousand years ago, walking through Galilee, Jesus had picked the pod off a mustard plant and opened it to reveal many tiny seeds. Taking one of the seeds and showing it to the people gathered around him Jesus explained that a little amount of faith, not the size of the pod but of one of the myriad of seeds it contained, was all that was needed to enter the kingdom of God. Seeds and sowers, ripe ears of corn and harvesters all had played their part in the storied metaphors told throughout human history to make the source of life, the ground of being, comprehensible. Jesus had spoken through stories, emphasizing the metaphoric value of familiar things and ordinary daily deeds. Vincent's sowers walking across the plowed field were continuing the tradition of storytelling, no longer confined to an oral one. Years before in the Borinage, the church authorities had dismissed Vincent for his allegedly poor oratory skills. This rebuke had led Vincent to speak through the power of the visual, the emblematic.

Vincent used the figure of Millet's sower in another painting: "The Artist on the Road to Tarascon." It is an image of his own likeness striding, like the sower, along a country lane, shouldering his easel and painting supplies instead of strewing seeds. It is the artist-sower who is symbolically spreading the seeds of a new art, an art through which suggestive colors were becoming a powerful means to satisfy the *yearning for the infinite.*

PAINTING PROMISES COLOR AND MUSIC

In everything there is now old gold, bronze, copper, one might say, and with that, the green azure of the sky heated white-hot produces a delicious color, exceedingly harmonious, with the broken tones as found in a Delacroix.

—Arles, June 12 or 13, 1888

Painting as it is now promises to become more subtle—more music and less sculpture—in fact, it promises color. As long as it keeps this promise.

—Arles, on or about August 26, 1888

Vincent painted a vineyard in the spring of 1888 under a blue sky—a tangle of verdant vines wildly reaching beyond the picture frame. "The Green Vineyard" is a solid statement that winter has passed and spring has arrived. The various shades of green and the pale and deep blues of the sky are symbolic for new growth, for the creative power in nature.

The changing of the seasons is something people are very sensitive to. For example, in a neighborhood like the Geest and in those courtyards of the so-called almshouses, the winter is always an anxious and difficult and frightening time, and spring a deliverance.

If one pays attention to it, one sees that such a first spring day is a kind of Gospel message.

—The Hague, February 8, 1883

Vincent imagined Theo looking onto this spring greenery when he received the shipment of canvases sent by train to Paris. Perhaps his brother might be delivered from the difficult winter months in the grey city by a message of spring, even in the form of a painting.

Vincent had written from Nuenen about his desire to be able to express the moods of the seasons by contrasting colors; he wondered about finding the right color to express a summer effect under the pale Dutch sun:

> [It was] *not easy to find a summer sun effect, which is as lush and as simple and as pleasant to look at as the characteristic effects of the other seasons.*
>
> *Spring is tender green (young corn) and pink (apple blossoms). Autumn is the contrast of the yellow leaves against violet tones. Winter is the snow with the small black silhouettes.*
>
> *But now, if summer is the contrast of blues against an element of orange in the golden bronze of the corn, in this way, one could do a painting with each of the contrasting complementary colors (red and green, blue and orange, yellow and violet, white and black) a painting which would express the moods of the seasons well.*
>
> —Nuenen, on or about July 2, 1884

In Arles, he succeeded in capturing the hot climate of the South, in painting the rich and simple mood of a summer sun effect. He had already painted the greening of spring and then the *wheat fields have been a reason for working, just like the orchards in bloom. And I barely have time to get ready for the next campaign, that of the vineyards* (Arles, on or about June 25, 1888). A vineyard during the grape harvest became a rich tapestry of warm oranges, reds and golden yellows with patches of the blue peasant smocks worn by the harvesters toiling under the last rays of a summer sun. "The Red Vineyard" is alive with the vibratory quality of the contrasting colors that Vincent had envisioned while still in the North. The shimmering heat of the late afternoon with the bright orb of the setting sun in a yellow sky radiates out into the space where the viewers of this "summer sun effect" are standing today, almost feeling and hearing the vibrating colors resounding in a powerful ode to joy.

When Vincent began using the intense new pigments in Paris, he paid more attention to the emotions, the seasonal effects and moods, and the "music" that could be created through the different combinations of colors in all their pure and broken tonal variations. He found that in certain works by artists who were "daring" with their colors, their paintings could be compared to music:

> *Dupré is perhaps even more of a colorist than Corot and Daubigny, although they both are that too, and Daubigny especially is very daring with his colors. But with Dupré there is something in his color of a splendid symphony, completed, willed, masculine; I suspect Beethoven to be something like that. . . . That symphony is surprisingly* CALCULATED *and yet simple and infinitely deep as nature is itself.*
>
> —Nuenen, mid-June, 1884

When Vincent wanted to create certain moods in his work, he used colors like a composer used the notes on a scale. Describing a particularly enticing scene, he wrote to Theo, *I can't paint as beautifully as that, but it absorbs me so much that I let myself go without thinking about any rule* (Arles, September 18, 1888). Using his brush, as a musician would move the bow on his violin, Vincent played variations on what nature spread before him, completely surrendering himself to the abundance of colors and shapes of the riotously flowering oleanders, the rich golden fields of wheat, and the cool greens of shaded glens. Through intensifying colors and emboldening lines, he wasn't just describing their physical appearance but was aiming at capturing their essence and intrinsic qualities. He gave color the autonomy, the power, to add an extra dimension that transcended the presence of his subject matter. Color, just as music, could be enjoyed without the necessity of any interpretation or theme:

> *So I am always between two currents of ideas, the first, the material difficulties, turning around and around to make a living; and then the study of color.*
>
> *I always hope to make a discovery there. To express the love of two lovers through a wedding of two complementary colors, their mixing and their opposition, the mysterious vibration of adjacent tones. To express the thought of a brow through the radiance of a light tone against a dark background. To express hope through some star; the ardor of a living being through the radiance of a setting sun. That is certainly not delusive realism, but isn't it something that really exists?*
>
> —Arles, September 3, 1888

Vincent was always on the lookout for new scenes to paint, but he equally sought models, always longing to connect with people. He had never stopped believing:

> [There is] *no better or shorter way to improve my work than to do figures. Also, I always feel confidence when doing portraits, knowing that that work is more serious—that's perhaps not the word—but rather it is what enables me to cultivate what's best and most serious in me.*
>
> —Arles, on or about August 3, 1888

He was critical of the great number of photographers who seemed to be very busy taking portraits, but whose work showed *always those same conventional eyes, noses, mouths—wax-like and smooth and cold. It always does remain DEAD.* Vincent felt that realist artists did not make banal imitations of life, but rather through their paintings provided a vision that could be more complete, more astounding, and more convincing than reality. The painted portraits would have *a life of their own that comes completely from the painter's soul, something the machine can't access* (Antwerp, December 14, 1885). Real people would be Vincent's subjects, but his emotional engagement with them, his intuition and experience, would provide a more enlightening view of their place in the world:

> [In a picture] *I want to say something consoling like a piece of music. I want to paint men and women with that something of the eternal which in the past was symbolized by the halo, and which we seek to convey by a radiance, through the vibration of our colorings.*
>
> —Arles, September 3, 1888

Vincent's friends in Arles, the bombastic postmaster Roulin and his wife and children, the innkeeper's wife memorialized as l'Arlesienne, the unassuming peasants in the fields, and the Zouave soldiers on leave became his "saints in modern dress." One such man was the farmer Patience Escalier. Using color arbitrarily in his portrait of him, Vincent looked at the man coming straight from his work in the fields:

> [from] *the very furnace of the height of harvest time, at high noon. Hence the orange colors blazing like red-hot iron, hence the luminous tones of old gold in the shadows. Oh, my dear brother, and the nice people will only see a caricature in this exaggeration, but what do we care? We've read* La Terre *and* Germinal, *and if we were painting a peasant, we would want to show that in the end what we have read has in some way become part of us.*
>
> —Arles, August 18, 1888

La Terre and *Germinal* by Emile Zola are uncompromisingly harsh and realistic stories about the lives of an itinerant farm worker and a miner, respectively. While based on his own observations and research, Zola used the artist's liberty to exaggerate in order to provide a more striking portrait of hardship and suffering. Instead of words, Vincent used colors to express what it was like to work in the furnace-like heat of a summer's day in the South of France. Vincent painted a very different mood in the portrait of an artist friend:

> [A man who] *dreams great dreams, who works as the nightingale sings, because that is his nature. This man will be blond. In this picture I would want to put my appreciation, my love I have for him. So I will paint him as he is, as faithfully as I can, to begin with. But the picture is not finished this way. To finish it I will now become the arbitrary colorist. I exaggerate the fairness of the hair, I arrive at orange tones, chromes and pale citron-yellow. Behind the head, instead of painting the dull wall of the shabby apartment, I paint infinity. I create a plain background of the richest, most intense blue that I can make, and through this simple combination, the blond head brightly lit against the rich blue background, I get a mysterious effect, like a star in the deep blue.*
>
> —Arles, August 18, 1888

An exact rendering of a portrait or a landscape scene could not convey the sensation the artist had while painting: *It is a color therefore not locally true from the point of view of the realist who creates an optical illusion, but a color suggesting some kind of emotion, a passionate temperament* (Arles, September 8, 1888). Suggestive colors, intensified color contrasts, and exaggerated, even distorted, lines and gestures could make a stronger and more essential statement.

> *But in the meantime I'm always fed by nature. I exaggerate, I sometimes make changes in the theme, but in the end I don't invent the whole content of the painting; on the contrary, I find it all completely there in nature—but it has to be disentangled.*
>
> —Arles, on or about October 5, 1888

This is what Vincent had done in his portrait of "The Potato Eaters." He had written about this image that it was one of the ugliest he had painted. He felt the same way about the scene of a public coffee house he created in Arles. This was a place that remained open all night and was often frequented by vagabonds and prostitutes or people too drunk to find their way home. Vincent experienced the squalor and ruinous effect of this place, where one could *go mad or commit a crime*. He stayed up several nights to paint an image that would *express, as it were, the power of darkness in a low public house . . . an atmosphere like a devil's furnace, of pale sulfur* (Arles, September 9, 1888). Using the effect of disharmoniously contrasting colors was the determining factor in creating the mood of this painting, "The Night Café on the Place Lamartine." He felt it was the *equivalent though different of "The Potato Eaters":*

> *With the red and the green I've tried to express the terrible human passions. The room is blood-red and dull yellow, a green billiard table in the centre, citron-yellow lamps with an orange and green glow. It's a battle and an antithesis everywhere of the most different shades of greens and reds; some purple and blue in the characters of the sleeping hooligans, seemingly small in the empty, high room. The blood-red and the green-yellow of the billiard table, for example, contrast with the little bit of delicate Louis XV green of the counter, where there's a pink bouquet. The white clothes of the owner, who is watching from a corner in this furnace, become citron-yellow, pale and luminous green.*
>
> —Arles, September 8, 1888

In contrast to "The Night Café," Vincent painted several images of his bedroom in Arles, an empty bedroom with a wooden bed and two chairs: *I wanted to arrive at an effect of simplicity as one finds it described in Felix Holt* [George Eliot novel]. He was also inspired by the Japanese who, he believed, *have lived in very simple interiors, and what great artists have lived in that country!* (Saint-Rémy, October 21, 1889). He aimed at a simplicity that despite bright colors had a calming effect:

> *This time it's simply my bedroom, only it is color that has to do the job here, and by giving, through its simplification, a greater style to things, to be suggestive here of rest or of sleep in general. In short, looking at the painting should give rest to the mind, or rather, to the imagination. . . .*
>
> *The shadows and cast shadows are removed; it's colored in flat, plain hues like in Japanese prints. It will contrast, for example, with the Tarascon diligence and the night café.*
>
> —Arles, October 16, 1888

The walls of a pale blue-violet and the perspective lines of the floor tiles have the effect of drawing the viewer into this space, to rest there for a while and recover.

The Nuenen "Still Life with Bible" had been Vincent's first hesitant attempt to experiment with the use of suggestive and symbolic colors. In his first painting of "The Sower" three years later he no longer held back in using the powerful dynamics and symbolism of color. The "Night Café" and the portraits of Patience Escalier and the poet friend followed in this style. Often Vincent exclaimed that his exaggerations were *dreadfully ugly and bad*, but then again when *I am moved by something, like now by this little article on Dostoyevsky, then these are the only ones that appear to have any deep meaning* (Arles, on or about September 11, 1888).

Vincent wrote to his sister Willemien in the fall of 1888:

> *It is my belief that one actually has to paint the rich and magnificent aspects of nature, we have a need of gaiety and happiness, of hope and love. The more ugly, old,*

mean, ill, poor I get, the more I want to make my revenge by creating a brilliant color, well-arranged, resplendent.

—Arles, between September 9 and 14, 1888

SORROWFUL YET ALWAYS REJOICING

The more I am spent, ill, a broken jug, the more I too become a creative artist in this great renaissance of art of which we speak.

These things are certainly so, but this eternally existing art and this renaissance, this green shoot growing from the roots of the old felled trunk, these are such spiritual things that a kind of melancholy remains within us when we think that one could have created life at less expense than creating art.

—Arles, July 29, 1888

Not long after arriving in Arles, Vincent had found a run-down house and he began to decorate it, so that everything about it was artful. He hoped that his "Yellow House" would become the "Studio du Midi," a place where like-minded artists could live together as brothers-in-arms. He imagined the Japanese artists to have formed such communities of collaboration and mutual support. Paul Gauguin was the only one to join Vincent in his Yellow House. It is in anticipation of his Parisian friend's arrival that Vincent painted the series of sunflowers that were to hang on the walls of his home. He had actually experimented with lithography in The Hague and had written: *No result of my work could make me happier than if ordinary working people would hang such prints in their homes* (The Hague, November 16 or 17, 1882). His sunflowers were paintings he also hoped to mass produce one day so that they could hang on the walls of homes everywhere, as did the ukiyo-e prints of the Japanese.

He also created a painting especially for Gauguin's room in which he transformed the view of an ordinary public garden into a place where one could find one's muse—"The Poet's Garden." He hoped that Gauguin looking at this painting would be inspired and not regret his decision to join Vincent in the South:

> *The mundane public garden contains plants and bushes that make one dream of landscapes in which one could easily picture Botticelli, Giotto, Petrarch, Dante, and Boccaccio. In the decoration I've tried to tease out the essence of what the changeless character of the region represents.*
>
> —Arles, October 3, 1888

Gauguin agreed to go to Arles in October of 1888, having secured financial support from Theo and a promise to have his paintings exhibited in Paris. Vincent and Gauguin lived together in the Yellow House for only three months—months filled with intense painting sessions and many heated arguments. Both artists often set up their easels in front of the same scenes; the resulting paintings speak vividly about their different approaches to art. While Vincent was intent on *teasing out the essence of the changeless character of the region,* Gauguin argued that they had to paint from memory. Challenged by Gauguin, Vincent painted his "Red Vineyard" in his studio from memory after having observed the harvesters at work. Gauguin's grape harvest, lacking vibrant color contrasts, is more about the toil and misery of the grape pickers. Gauguin believed that it was the artist's task to enlarge the things of life into the proportions of a myth, whereas Vincent saw the myths and parables in the most down-to-earth and ordinary. Through close observation of reality, he sought to reveal how much divinity shone through every sunlit landscape and laboring peasant.

Vincent never attained the collegiality with Gauguin that he had hoped for. By December the tensions between them became so intolerable that Gauguin announced he would return to Paris. This threat of abandonment and the emotional upheaval and tension of the previous three months unsettled Vincent. In the week before Christmas, Vincent suffered a major nervous crisis, during which part of his ear was severed. Discovered in his bed in the Yellow House, unconscious and bleeding profusely, he was rushed to the "Hotel de Dieu," the hospital in Arles. What happened has always been unclear. A story circulated that Vincent had inflicted the wound himself and then wrapped the severed part of his ear in paper and brought it to a prostitute. Vincent gave no clear explanations in his letters to Theo about the incident, just veiled references to a story by Alphonse Daudet. In that book, he said, Theo would find some insight into Gauguin's character. Vincent also wrote that Gauguin asked him to send his fencing equipment, which, in his hurry to leave Arles, he had left behind. To this Vincent added, *I for one am quite decided to go on being armed with nothing but my brush and my pen* (Arles, January 1889). It appears that both Gauguin and Vincent had come to an agreement never to mention what happened in Arles that December.

There was, and still is, a strong bullfighting tradition in Arles. Once the matador has killed the bull, he cuts off the ear of his victim and presents it to his lady. One can only conjecture that Vincent may have been familiar with this custom. Vincent's dream to establish the Studio du Midi in Arles had been effectively "killed" by Gauguin's departure. Presenting his severed ear to a prostitute he knew mirrored the matador's gestures in the final act of the spectacle.

Already prone to bouts of melancholy and anxiety, the drama that had taken place in the Yellow House marked the beginning of the reoccurring seizures that would plague Vincent for the rest of his life. For the next few months, Vincent had to be admitted to the Arles hospital several times. He experienced physical weakness and seizures, and suffered from loneliness, and failure: *I can't precisely describe what it is that I have, there sometimes are terrible fits of anxiety—without any apparent cause—or then a feeling of emptiness and fatigue in my head* (Arles, between April 28 and May 2, 1889). During times of calm and recovery while still in the hospital, Vincent did the only thing that kept him from falling into complete despair—he painted. A young intern with modern ideas realized that this patient needed to be involved with the process of his own healing. Vincent painted the inner courtyard of the hospital and made a study of the interior of the fever ward. When he was well enough to leave the hospital, he went out into the orchards that were blooming once again. This time he painted the flowering trees seen from a distance behind dark vertical tree trunks looming in the foreground, almost like bars on a window. These gnarly blackened tree trunks are what the eye initially perceives when seeing the painting for the first time. But spending a bit longer before it, one notices through the barricade of trunks an orchard of flowering trees with a small figure walking among them. Vincent challenges the eyes of the viewer to look beyond the obstructing trees, just as he forced himself to look beyond his present difficulties and sorrows for signs of joy and hope.

He had read the story *Candide* by Voltaire, which contains a philosophical treatise on optimism versus pessimism. Vincent's reading once again encouraged and inspired him to surmount his suffering. He incorporated the philosophy into his own thinking and wrote: *For the time being there's every reason to say, with père Pangloss* [character in *Candide*], *all is for the best in the best of possible worlds* (Arles, between April 28 and May 2, 1889). While Voltaire meant the words by Pangloss to be ironic, Vincent took them to heart. Painting flowering trees and wheat fields, and all the glorious aspects of nature was essential for Vincent's efforts to see the good in all circumstances. Despite the menacing problems in life, there was still *a springtime of greenery*, full of promise. This attitude reaffirmed his favorite biblical phrase: "Sorrowful, yet always rejoicing" (2 Corinthians 6:10). It was a phrase the two brothers often cited in their letters to each other.

By the spring of 1890, the people of Arles, who felt the strange Dutch painter was a troublemaker whose erratic behavior appeared threatening, no longer tolerated Vincent in their midst. Based on a petition signed by a group of citizens, his Yellow House was boarded up and Vincent lost his home and studio. Though once again a stranger on the earth he was too ill to travel far. He had heard about a mental asylum in the little town of Saint-Rémy a few miles away. Going to this place, an old monastery called Saint-Paul de Mausole, was the only alternative he had. So he packed up his easel and paints and left Arles, alone and filled with remorse and uncertainty. He had spent a little over a year there and it had been a prolific time. Vincent had created about one hundred drawings and more than two hundred paintings that he had sent to Theo. Further, he had found time to read many books and write more than two hundred letters, most of them to Theo. More than ever he relied on this bond with his younger brother; it had become almost his only link to the outside world. Now, accompanied by Theo's love, along with his tireless financial and moral support, Vincent entered the asylum of Saint-Paul de Mausole.

10

Saint-Rémy: The Language of Nature

Never have I felt so peaceful as here and in the hospital in Arles—to be able to paint a little at last. Quite near here there are some little gray and blue mountains, and below them are some very, very green cornfields and pines.

—Saint-Rémy, May 9, 1889

I have a little room with greenish-gray paper with two curtains of sea-green with a print of very pale roses, enlivened by slight traces of blood-red. These curtains, probably left here by some rich and ruined deceased, are very pretty in design. Probably from the same source comes a very worn armchair; it is upholstered with a tapestry mottled like a Díaz or a Monticelli: brown, red, pink, white, cream, black, forget-me-not blue, and bottle-green.

—Saint-Rémy, on or about May 23, 1889

The monastery of Saint-Paul de Mausole in Saint-Rémy had been built in the Middle Ages. For the last few hundred years, it had opened its doors to people with mental disorders. In the absence of psychiatric hospitals, monasteries throughout Europe had frequently become safe havens for the mentally unstable, the destitute, and the outcast. Vincent signed himself into the asylum of Saint-Paul de Mausole of his own free will. Once again he was fortunate to come into the care of a progressive caretaker, a doctor who believed that his patients needed, if possible, to remain occupied with meaningful and purposeful work to help them attain some stability in their lives. In this sanctuary, Vincent was given a room in which to sleep and another in which to paint and store his paint supplies. All cell-like rooms were furnished sparsely and had bars on their windows:

> *I wanted to tell you that I think I have done well to come here; first of all by seeing the reality of the life of the different madmen or lunatics in this menagerie, I am losing the vague dread, the fear of the thing. And little by little I can come to see that madness is an illness like any other. Then the change of surroundings, I imagine, does me good. . . .*
>
> *The idea of duty to work is coming back to me very strongly, and I think that my ability to work will come back to me fairly quickly. Only work often absorbs me so much that I think I shall always remain absent-minded and awkward in fending for myself for the rest of my life.*
>
> —Saint-Rémy, May 9, 1889

Vincent wrote a lot about his condition and found that he shared some of the same symptoms as several of the other inmates. Comparing the anxiety that his illness caused with living a miner's life, he wrote:

> *I really think M. Peyron is right when he says that, strictly speaking, I am not mad, for my mind is absolutely normal and clear in between times and even more so than before. But during the crises it is terrible, and then I lose consciousness of everything. But that spurs me on to work and to seriousness, like a miner who makes haste in what he does because he is always in danger.*
>
> —Saint-Rémy, October 8, 1889

In time, Vincent formed tenuous friendships with those with whom he now shared his daily life:

> *Because even though there are some who howl or rave habitually, there is much real friendship here that one has for each other. They say we must put up with others so that others will put up with us and other very sound reasoning, which they accordingly put into practice. And between ourselves we understand each other very well; I can, for instance, sometimes chat with one of them who can only reply with incoherent sounds, because he is not afraid of me.*
>
> —Saint-Rémy, on or about May 23, 1889

A ROOM WITH A VIEW

> *Through the iron-barred window I can see a square field of wheat in an enclosure, in a perspective like a Van Goyen* [Dutch artist], *above which I see the sun rising in all its glory in the morning.*
>
> —Saint-Rémy, on or about May 23, 1889

Even though there were bars on his windows, Vincent gained a new freedom. In a safe environment where his needs were taken care of, he was at liberty to observe and, during recovery between seizures, to paint. He had learned to look beyond obscuring troubles—gazing between the bars of the windows he saw a wheat field enclosed by a wall. The wheat was young and green in the spring of his arrival in Saint-Rémy. Beyond the walls of the enclosed wheat field, Vincent could see the undulating lines of the purple colored Alpilles, *that chain of little hills perfumed with thyme and lavender; neither very difficult nor very high, which form a horizon of blue waves to the Provencal roads.* He witnessed many a hopeful sunrise over the wheat field and the blue horizon line:

> *This morning a long time before sunrise I saw the countryside from my window, with nothing but the morning star, which looked very big. Daubigny and Rousseau have done it, however, with the expression of intimacy and vast peace and majesty that this has, yet adding a feeling so heartbreaking, so personal. I do not detest emotions like that.*
>
> —Saint-Rémy, between May 31 and June 6, 1889

From his room Vincent could follow the path of the sun throughout the four seasons. He was to stay in Saint-Rémy for exactly one year during which he memorialized the enclosed field of the asylum in all its stages of growth, from the verdant plants to the ripe gold harvest. He could once again observe sowers and reapers toiling away. His painting of a reaper reached the same parable-like depth as "The Sower" done in Arles—it too pointed to something deeper through the ordinary act of harvesting:

> *I then saw in this reaper, a vague figure struggling like a devil in intense heat to get to the end of his toil, I then saw the image of death, in the sense that humanity would be the wheat being reaped. So it is, if you like, the opposite of that sower I tried doing before. But in this death there is nothing sad, it goes on in full daylight with a sun flooding everything in a light of pure gold. . . . It is an image of death as is spoken in the great book of nature, but what I have sought is the "almost smiling." It is all yellow except for a line of violet hills, a yellow pale and blond. I find that funny myself, that I saw it like that through the iron bars of a cell.*
>
> —Saint-Rémy, September 5 and 6, 1889

The traditional symbolism of the reaper is death. Vincent did not view this figure as pointing to the end of life, but rather showed him to be very much a part of the totality of life, indicating a passage from one half of existence to the *other hemisphere of life*. Vincent thought much about his mortality as he suffered the "almost dying" experiences of his seizures. In several letters he wrote that it would be so simple and could explain so well *the atrocities of life that now overwhelm and distress us so if life had another, second hemisphere, invisible for sure, but where we go to when we take our last breath* (Arles, July 31, 1888):

> *That stirs up the eternal question: Is life visible to us in its entirety or do we know of only one hemisphere before we die?*
>
> *Painters—to speak only of them—being dead and buried, speak to a following generation or to several following generations through their works. Is that all, or is there possibly even more? In the life of a painter, perhaps death may not be the most difficult thing.*
>
> *I myself declare not to know anything about it. But always, the sight of the stars makes me dream as simply as the black dots on the map that represent towns and villages make me dream. Why, I say to myself, should the bright dots in the firmament be less accessible to us than the black dots on the map of France?*
>
> *If we take the train to go to Tarascon or Rouen, then we take death to go to a star. What is certainly true in this reasoning is that while we are alive, we cannot reach a star any more than once dead we could take the train. Therefore, it does not seem impossible that cholera, kidney stones, consumption, or cancer could be celestial means of locomotion, just as steamboats, omnibuses, and the railway are terrestrial ones. To die peacefully of old age would be to go there on foot.*
>
> —Arles, July 9 or 10, 1888

> *Science or scientific reasoning, seems to me to be an instrument that will take us quite far in the future.*

> *Because look, one thought that the earth was flat and that was true—it still is today—from Paris to Asnières, for example. But that didn't prevent science from proving that the earth, is above all, round. Nowadays nobody contests that.*
>
> *However, at present, and despite that, we still believe that life is flat and goes from birth to death. But life too is probably round and far superior in scope and possibilities to the single hemisphere that we know at present. Future generations, probably, will enlighten us on this most interesting subject, and then science itself could, no offense, reach conclusions more or less parallel to Christ's words with respect to the other half of existence.*
>
> *Whatever the case, the fact is that we are painters in reality, and it is a matter of breathing one's breath as long as one has breath.*
>
> —Arles, June 26, 1888

While breathing his breath, Vincent could soar in spirit beyond the bars of his window and participate, with his brush and paints, in the moods of the landscape and in the toil of the seasonal laborers. And all that he saw and felt he captured with his energetic lines and resounding color symphonies.

THE INNER GARDENS

> *And if it were not that I have almost a double nature, that of a monk and that of a painter, I would have been, long ago, reduced completely and fully to the condition of madness. . . . Yet, even so, I do not think that my madness is a fear of persecution, since my feelings when I am in a state of excitement lead me rather to the concerns for eternity and eternal life.*
>
> —Arles, October 21, 1888

Medieval monasteries contained within their walls gardens where monks spent time in contemplation and prayer. Once people in need of solace and recuperation began to be admitted, walking and resting in these gardens became an integral part of their treatment. Medical treatises in the nineteenth century encouraged the exposure of patients to nature for their mental, spiritual, and physical healing.

In the enclosed inner gardens of the monastery Vincent became a truer contemplative. He sat on benches under ivy-covered trees and flowering lilac bushes and meditated, with pen or brush in hand. He crouched down among the irises and painted them as if he were one of them, face-to-face. The restorative atmosphere of the cool shaded garden plants appear on his canvases just as he must have experienced them. Looking at his paintings today, one can almost sense the air of the fragrant shadows and relish the calming effect of the greens and lavenders. He wrote about finding his "paradou," the paradise-like garden mentioned in Emile Zola's book *The Demise of Father Mouret*. In this story, a fallen parish priest finds spiritual rejuvenation in a walled-in garden that Zola described with painterly insight. Zola's words and Vincent's paintings succeed in conveying the same atmosphere of a lush garden sanctuary. Sitting among the vibrant garden growth, Vincent's contemplation of eternity and eternal life found expression and relevance in the act of painting the very nature that surrounded him. These meditations grounded him and helped him regain his balance after each severe seizure. Vincent's "paradou" paintings are invitations to enter into a garden and stay there a while, letting nature arouse feelings of peace and comfort.

BEYOND THE WALLS

By working diligently from nature without saying beforehand, I want to do this or that, by working as if making a pair of shoes, without artistic preoccupations,

> *one will not always do well, but on the days one least expects it, one will find a motif that can hold its own with the work of those who have gone before us. One learns to get to know a country that is basically quite different from what it appeared to be at first sight.*
>
> —Saint-Rémy, November 26, 1889

> *One needs a certain dose of inspiration, a ray from on high that is not from within ourselves, in order to do beautiful things. When I had done those sunflowers, I looked for the opposite and yet the equivalent, and I said—it is the cypress.*
>
> —Saint-Rémy, February 1, 1890

When Vincent felt strong and well enough, he was given an attendant and could go beyond the walls of the asylum to explore the country surrounding Saint-Rémy. Carrying his easel and paint supplies, he wandered through the olive groves and fields bordered by cypresses, and there, enveloped by the entire splendor, he painted with the same intensity as before. Wherever he went he saw evocative metaphors. Everything affected him deeper, more sensually and emotionally than before. He felt the mystery of the ancient olive trees, the exultation of the cypresses in their skyward reach, and the force of germination in the fertile fields around him. He became more attuned to the presence of a spiritual energy that infused the physical world. The subjects Vincent painted were beyond descriptive or narrative images; Vincent had succeeded, as the Zen poet Basho wrote, in becoming "one with nature." When he painted the hills and the clouds, it was the hills and the clouds whose essence spoke on his canvases. Sun-covered hills, glowing wheat fields, olive trees shimmering in the heat of the day, flaming cypresses, and radiant people all spoke their own wordless language. This was a language of symbol and allegory, personal yet at the same time universal. He had found such an art language in the work of Nicolas Poussin, who was a *painter who thinks and makes one think about everything, in whose paintings all reality is at the same time a symbol* (Nuenen, October 4, 1885). For Vincent to render a reality that was at the same time symbolic was to render the reality that he experienced through all of his senses, through his knowledge of things, through his intuition and through his love. This reality involved him totally. He painted with his whole being: body, mind, and soul.

While wandering in the surrounding environment of the asylum he came upon an abandoned quarry and a steep ravine. Inherent in both images is a sense of struggle. In the painting of the abandoned quarry we see a bottomless, dark, gaping cave where a figure is barely visible. It is a place of total abandonment, a place of Vincent's own descent into the oblivion of his seizures. The viewer himself is engulfed in the quarry, with no horizon line and sunlit sky to offer hope and deliverance. Just as in Drenthe, Vincent had found in nature places that mirrored the drama of his own experience. The painting of the ravine brings to mind the metaphor used in Psalm 23, where the psalmist is comforted by knowing that even in the "ravine as dark as death" there was nothing to fear, for God was at his side. In Vincent's painting, there are two figures struggling to make it through a steep, rocky gorge alongside a turbulent stream. Vincent knew the psalm, and in his moments of intense physical strain and recovery from his seizures, it may have felt like fighting to make it through a dark, deep abyss. By painting two figures emerging from the ravine, Vincent figuratively portrayed the conviction that even in the intense moments of agony one was not alone. The narratives on his canvasses, while using observed reality, almost became his own story. He had done a study of the ravine on the day the mistral was blowing and had had to wedge his easel in between large stones. Even painting this image was a struggle. Through his sensitivity and contemplative gazing at the natural world, Vincent saw in the glorious aspects of sun-drenched fields, as well as in the dark deep ravines, the presence of the "Something on High."

Wheat fields, as in Arles, surrounded Saint-Rémy. Vincent painted them over and over again in all stages of growth. Contemplating fields, or just a simple blade of grass or a pine tree branch (Saint-Rémy, July 2, 1889), could calm his mental strain and anxiety:

> *Now comparing people with grains of wheat: every person who is healthy and natural has, as in a grain of wheat, within themselves the power to germinate. And thus natural life is about germination. What the power to germinate is in a grain of wheat, that is love in us.*
>
> —Paris, late October, 1887

The symbolic meaning of wheat, from its seeds to the tall yellow stalks and sheaves, had provided Vincent with metaphors and meaning from his earliest days walking through the Brabant fields. Likening the "power to germinate" in every kernel of wheat to the force of love in human beings made a whole field of wheat a very powerful place. Standing before such a field, or looking at it even in the form of a painting, was a firm reminder of the presence of a creative force, a force that encompassed all of creation. The "Something on High," the creative force of love, was not found in religions "which pass away," but in the simple things of life:

> *Learning to suffer without complaining, learning to consider pain without repugnance, it is precisely there that one risks vertigo a little. Could it be possible, however, one could see even a vague probability that on the other side of life we will perceive good reasons for pain, which seen from down here sometimes takes up the whole horizon so that it achieves the despairing proportions of a deluge. Of that we know very little, of proportions,*

> *and it is better to look at a wheat field, even in the form of a painting.*
>
> —Saint-Rémy, July 2, 1889

Gazing at the fields of wheat in Arles, Saint-Rémy, and soon in Auvers-sur-Oise, was never just a matter of enjoying the scenery, but always the source of comfort, hope, and strength.

SYMBOLS OF THE DIVINE

> *And nevertheless to feel the stars and the infinite high and clear above. Then life is almost enchanted after all. Oh! Those who don't believe in this sun here are real infidels.*
>
> —Arles, August 18, 1888

> *If I stay here I would not try to paint a Christ in the Garden of Olives, but in fact the olive harvest as it is still seen today, and then, rendering the correct proportions of the human figure in it would perhaps make one think of it all the same.*
>
> —Saint-Rémy, on or about November 19, 1889

Vincent judged paintings from a painter's point of view and looked for the expressive quality, for the honesty and authentic feeling of the artist in each picture. In Saint-Rémy during the weeks when he was too weak to paint outside, he reverted to copying the prints of those artists in whose works he found such qualities:

> *I place the black and white prints by Delacroix or Millet or something made after their work in front of me as a subject. And then I improvise color on it, but of course not quite being me, but searching for memories of their pictures. But the memory, the vague consonance of colors that are in the sentiment, if not true, that is my*

> *own interpretation. A lot of people do not copy, a lot of others do. I started on it accidentally and I find that it teaches, and above all sometimes consoles me. And then my brush goes between my fingers as a bow would on the violin and absolutely for my pleasure.*
>
> —Saint-Rémy, on or about September 20, 1889

Rembrandt's "Raising of Lazarus" took on a deeper meaning for Vincent when he began experiencing his agonizing seizures. The painting is based on the biblical story of Jesus summoned to the tomb of Lazarus by his two sisters with the hope that their brother could be brought back to life. The figure of Jesus with a hand raised in blessing stands above the grave of the lifeless Lazarus, his body wrapped in a shroud. The two sisters, Martha and Mary, lean over his grave with outstretched hands. In his copy, Vincent replaced Rembrandt's figure of Jesus with a brilliantly radiating sun. Vincent had never seen the figure of Jesus, but believed from reading the Bible that Jesus was the Light of the World. The symbol for this light was the enlivening and illuminating power of the sun. He had not seen Lazarus, but he identified with being almost buried when his seizures left him unconscious. And he knew what it felt like to be consoled by caring friends. Thus Vincent painted Lazarus in his likeness. Mary and Martha were portrayed as the two women in Arles who had treated him with compassion and kindness. In Vincent's painting, the divine radiance of the Light of the World empowers the women with a healing force that flows through their outstretched hands to Lazarus—Vincent. The compassionate touch of a human gesture empowered by a "ray from on high" was the experience Vincent had had; it was also the expression of his need for healing, comfort, and reconciliation. Vincent's copies of Delacroix's and Rembrandt's paintings are his only "religious paintings" with biblical content, but they are charged with his emotion and personal experience. Copying these works helped him *have a basis in these artists, and then produce the little I'm capable of in the same direction* (Saint-Rémy, September 10, 1889). Bringing their work into a personal context strengthened the bond he had always felt with them.

In Arles, Vincent had made an attempt to paint a scene directly from the Gospel. But he scraped the painted image off his canvas twice. He had intended it to be a study of Christ with the angel in the Garden of Olives:

> *Because here I can see real olives trees. But I cannot or rather I will not paint without models anymore. But I have the thing in my head with color: the starry night, the figure of Christ in blue, the strongest blues, and the angel blended with citron-yellow. And all the purples, from a blood-red purple to ashen in the landscape.*
>
> —Arles, September 21, 1888

He never completed such a painting. But he did paint the theme of agony and struggle, and of deliverance. These were emotions he had experienced and seen himself: the agony of his violent seizures and the struggle expressed in contorted trunks and branches of ancient olive trees; his relief at recovering from a time of despair and the glory of a sunrise over the dark rim of the horizon. As for the colors of "strongest blues" and "citron-yellow" and the image of a "starry night" he had had in his head to paint, these would appear on a canvas while in Saint-Rémy. The canvas he painted was "Starry Night," a star-filled sky above a "blood-red purple to ashen" landscape, one of the few that he created from memory.

Vincent was very critical of his friend Emile Bernard's attempt to paint his religious version of Christ agonizing in the Garden of Gethsemane amid the olive trees. He wrote to Theo:

> *Friend Bernard has probably never seen an olive tree. So then he avoids entertaining the least idea of the possible and of the reality of thing, and that is not the way to create.* No, *never have I got mixed up with their bibli-*

> *cal interpretations. I said that Rembrandt and Delacroix had done this admirably.*
>
> —Saint-Rémy, on or about November 19, 1889

Vincent wrote to Bernard that the gnarled and twisted olive trees gave a better, more truthful picture of "agony" than Bernard's imaginary Christ in an imagined garden of olive trees. Vincent added that it was the truth he adored and the possible, rather than abstractions. His own ambitions were limited *to a few clods of earth, some sprouting wheat, a cypress, an olive grove* (Arles, on or about November 26, 1889) through which, if he chose to do so, religious fervor could be expressed. He described two canvases that he felt were successful in conveying emotions of anxiety, or of calmness and peace:

> *You'll understand that this combination of red ochre, of green saddened with grey, of black lines that define the outlines, this produces somewhat the feeling of anxiety from which some of my companions in misfortune often suffer, and that one calls 'seeing red'. And by the way, the motif of the great tree struck by lightning, the sickly green and pink smile of the last autumn flower, confirm this idea. Another canvas shows a sun rising over a field of young wheat. The fleeing lines of the furrows lead high up on the canvas towards a wall and a range of lilac hills. The field is violet and yellow-green. The white sun is surrounded by a large yellow halo. Here, in contrast to the other canvas, I have tried to express calmness, a great peace.*
>
> *I am speaking to you of these two canvases, especially of the first, to remind you that in order to give an impression of anxiety, one can try to do it without aiming straight for the historical garden of Gethsemane. In order to render a consoling and gentle theme, it is not necessary to portray the characters from the Sermon*

> *on the Mount—Ah—it is no doubt wise, right, to be moved by the Bible, but modern reality has such a hold on us that even when we attempt abstractly to reconstruct ancient times in our thoughts, just then even the small events of our lives tear us away from these meditations, and our own adventures throw us forcibly into our personal feelings of joy, boredom, suffering, anger, or smiles. The Bible—the Bible—Millet was brought up on it since childhood, used to read only that book and yet never, or almost never, made biblical paintings.*
>
> —Arles, on or about November 26, 1889

Vincent doubted that Bernard based his paintings of Christ on an in-depth study of scriptures. Bernard's attempt at painting scenes from the Gospel story expressed a superficial religiosity and were artificial and affected. Seeing one of Bernard's Nativity scenes Vincent exclaimed:

> [It is] *too great an impossibility to believe a birth like that, right there on the road, the mother who begins to pray instead of to nurse, the fat ecclesiastical frogs kneeling as if in an epileptic fit are there. God knows how and why, but I myself don't find this healthy.*
>
> —Arles, on or about November 26, 1889

Vincent went on to cite the example of a Millet study that made him tremble and bow down to it—*peasants carrying to the farmhouse a calf born in the fields*. This was real, the stuff of which the biblical parables spoke. Bernard should read and study the whole Bible, or not at all. It wasn't an easy reading but one that saddened, stirred up despair and indignation:

> [It] *thoroughly distresses us, outraged by its pettiness and its contagious folly,* [yet] *the consolation which is contained in it, like a kernel inside a hard shell, a bitter pulp, is Christ. The figure of Christ has only been painted—as*

I feel it—by Delacroix and by Rembrandt. . . . and then Millet has painted . . . Christ's doctrine.

The rest makes me smile a little—the rest of religious painting—from the religious point of view, not from the painting point of view. Christ alone . . . lived serenely as an artist greater than all artists, disdaining marble and clay and paint, working in living flesh, that is, this extraordinary artist, almost unconceivable with the obtuse instrument of our nervous and stunted modern brains, made neither statues nor paintings nor even books . . . he states it forcibly . . . he made . . . living men, immortals. That's serious, you know, especially because it is the truth. . . .

Though this great artist—Christ—disdained writing books on ideas and feelings, he certainly disdained much less the spoken word, the parable above all. (What a sower, what a harvest, what a fig tree, etc.!) . . .

These reflections, my dear old Bernard take us a long way—a very long way—they raise us above art itself. They enable us to foresee the art of making life, the art of being immortal—alive. . . .

Nevertheless our own real life is humble indeed, our life as painters. Stagnating under the staggering yoke of the exertion of a craft almost impossible to carry out on this hostile planet, on the surface of which "love of art makes one lose real love."

—Arles, June 26, 1888

THE COMMON BOND

Look here, the question that comes to my mind is this one: Who are the human beings who actually live among

> *the olive, the orange and the lemon orchards? The peasant from there is someone different from the inhabitant of Millet's wide wheat fields. But Millet has opened our minds so that we become aware of the one who dwells in nature.*
>
> —Auvers-sur-Oise, May 25, 1890

In Saint-Rémy, Vincent's art was charged with movement and a greater intensity. His lines expressed individual intention and feeling and at the same time they seem to pulsate with a cosmic, rhythmic energy. *Where these lines are close and deliberate it begins to be a picture, even if it is exaggerated* (Saint-Rémy, September 10, 1889). He worked more rapidly, always changing shapes and colors where necessary, *exaggerating the essence of things* (Arles, May 26, 1888) in order to render a more truthful dimension of what he saw and felt. It was no longer a conscious labored decision what color to use, what line of perspective to draw, or where to put the horizon line—he drew and painted without measuring, just letting his pen or brush move over the canvas. *I have a terrible lucidity at moments . . . and the picture comes to me as in a dream* (Arles, September 25, 1888). In "Starry Night," the sky and stars, the hills and cypresses, the church spire and village cottages, the great and small, the insignificant and magnificent, became part of the same vital, creative energy field of lines and swirls. Feeling homesick for the North, he painted the church spire of a small Dutch village surrounded by the cypress trees and the little alps of Provence, whose "blue waves" continue in the undulating lines and swirls of the sky above. Earth and sky seem to merge. Visible brush strokes surge, roll, rise, and fall in rhythmic lines of blues and violet, of hills and sky. The vault of heaven, enlivened by citron-yellow swirls and spirals of sun, moon, and stars, is alive with the vibrations of sound and color. *At night,* Vincent wrote from Amsterdam years before, when *the sounds cease, God's voice is heard under the stars* (Amsterdam, September 18, 1877). In "Starry Night,"

Vincent made visible his understanding of a voice sounding through nature. From his readings of the Old Testament, Vincent knew that Creation was a speech event, it literally sounded forth: "In the beginning was the Word"—the sound of song that emanated and vibrated with life. Vincent used his language of art to do what he had set out to do in the Borinage as a young missionary: to speak of God's incarnation and presence in the world. From The Hague he had written:

> *There is at times something indescribable in those aspects—it is as if the whole of nature is speaking—and when one goes home one has the feeling as if one has just read a book by Victor Hugo, for example. As for me, I cannot understand that not everybody sees it and feels it. Doesn't nature or God do it for everyone who has eyes and ears and a heart to understand? It seems to me that a painter is happy, because he lives in harmony with nature, as soon as he can express, to some extent, what he sees.*
>
> —The Hague, November 26 and 27, 1882

Vincent's interwoven brush strokes and agrarian parables convey the reality that everything exists in relation to everything else. His figure of "The Reaper," for example, is engulfed within the golden wheat field. His presence is subtle; he is woven into the fabric of the stalks of wheat. Vincent lived how he painted these scenes: wholly absorbed by nature, by feeling the toil and labor of the reaper, even though he himself was not a reaper; by feeling the strain and stress of knotted roots; by recognizing the force in the germinating power of each kernel of wheat as an expression of love. His visible brush strokes became an extension of his understanding that he and the rest of the universe were not separate entities but all part of the same created whole. In the Borinage, he had wanted to follow the example of Christ. In Saint-Rémy, he became one with Christ in his purpose and "duty" to proclaim in a visible and universal language that the love and life of the Creator was present and continuously creating in the here and now. In his paintings of the *magnificent aspects of nature*, Vincent used the language of nature to express that it was nature that manifested the divine.

VINCENT'S SUNS RISING ABOVE THE ART WORLD

While in Saint-Remy Vincent was invited to exhibit some of his paintings at the annually occurring "Salon des Vingt," organized by a group of twenty Belgian artists who sought twenty international artists to join them. This exhibition led to the only sale of one of Vincent's artworks during his lifetime, "The Red Vineyard." Vincent's inclusion in the "Salon des Vingt" caught the attention of a young art critic, Albert Aurier. He published articles in the French periodical *Mercure de France* ("Les isolés: Vincent van Gogh," January 1890), as well as in the Belgian magazine *L'Art Moderne,* praising Vincent's "strange, intense and feverish work," while lamenting that Vincent van Gogh would never be completely understood by "the contemporary bourgeois mind." He characterized Vincent as a "dreamer, an exalted believer, a devourer of beautiful Utopias," finding his "palette incredibly dazzling" and his brushstrokes "fiery, very powerful and full of tension." Theo sent the articles to Vincent, who mulled over the words of praise and found them undeserved. To his sister Willemien he wrote:

> *I found the article by Mr. Aurier, leaving aside whether I merit what he says of me, in itself quite artistic, quite interesting, but it is rather as one should be, instead of the sad reality in which I sense myself to be.*
>
> *I wrote to him that in any case it seems to me that Monticelli and Gauguin are more like that, that it seemed therefore that what I deserve would be only secondary,*

> *very secondary. The ideas of which he speaks are not mine, for in general the Impressionist artists are all like that, under the same influence, and we are all rather somewhat neurotic. That is what makes us so sensitive to color and to its particular language, its complementary, contrasting, and harmonious effects.*
>
> *But when I read the article, I became almost sad, just by thinking: I ought to be like that, and I feel so inferior. And pride like drink intoxicates, when one is praised and one has been drinking one becomes sad, or anyway I am not sure how to say what I feel, but it seems to me that one would make better work if one created it within a family, without praising oneself.*
>
> —Saint-Rémy, February 19, 1890

Vincent wrote to Albert Aurier, to express his appreciation but also his sense that others were more deserving of his praise. He asked Theo:

> [Ask] *Mr. Aurier to not write anymore articles about my paintings, make the case in point that he, first of all, is wrong about me, and that in reality I feel much too damaged by grief to be able to deal with publicity. I am distracted by creating paintings, but if I hear them being talked about, it upsets me more than he knows.*
>
> —Saint-Rémy, April 29, 1890

Albert Aurier had opened the door to let a glimmer of Vincent's suns to escape. The "mind of the bourgeois" was beginning to expand to comprehend the idiom of Vincent's art.

11

Auvers-sur-Oise: The Harvest

Ah well, really, we can only make our pictures speak.

—Auvers-sur-Oise, July 23, 1890

New wheat was greening once again in the walled-in garden, when Vincent was summoned by Theo to return to the North. Theo had married and celebrated the birth of a son. Vincent had written to him:

> *Do you know what I hope for, once I let myself begin to hope? It is that a family will be for you what nature, the clods of earth, the grass, the yellow wheat, the peasant, are for me. That is to say, that you may find in your love for people not only the reason to work, but also the source of comfort and restoration when there is need for it.*
>
> —Saint-Rémy, September 5 and 6, 1889

But Theo himself was ailing. He was also filled with worries about Vincent's condition and seclusion far away in the Saint-Rémy asylum. Artist friends helped Theo connect with a doctor in the town of Auvers-sur-Oise, north of Paris, who was willing to take Vincent on as his patient. Vincent, now strong enough and also yearning to be closer to Theo, once again packed his painting supplies and boarded a train, this time heading North.

Stepping off the train in Auvers-sur-Oise, a little town northwest of Paris, Vincent was greeted by the familiar sight of wheat fields all around. He found a room in a small inn, where he was to stay for seventy days. During that period he painted over seventy paintings and made many drawings. He formed a friendship with his physician, Dr. Gachet, an eccentric who suffered from fits of melancholy. According to Vincent, Dr. Gachet was in more need of medical care than he was. And as always, with his paints and supplies, he walked about town and through the fields beyond looking for subjects to paint. He delighted in seeing thatched cottages, reminding him again of the weavers' huts. He also discovered that the artist Charles Daubigny had lived and recently died in Auvers. Daubigny too had painted the Auvers landscapes, and Daubigny's garden became the subject of Vincent's last paintings. He had come full circle: finding similarities to the Brabant of his youth and setting up his easel outside the home of the admired artist who had, like him, also spent time in the wilderness of Drenthe—the place where Vincent had committed himself fully to a life solely devoted to art.

Vincent painted the landscape surrounding Auvers over and over again:

> *For my part, I am quite absorbed in the immense plain with wheat fields against the hills, large as a sea, delicate yellow, delicate soft green, the delicate violet of a dug-up and weeded piece of ground, patterned at regular intervals with the green of flowering potato plants, everything under a sky of delicate blue, white, pink, violet tones.*
>
> —Auvers-sur-Oise, between July 10 and 14, 1890

Suffering from his intermittent seizures and worrying that he was a burden for Theo, he saw in the grey clouds over the fields an image of his own melancholy and suffering: *They are vast expanses of wheat under troubled skies, and I was not prevented from trying to express sadness and extreme loneliness* (Auvers-sur-Oise, on or about July 10, 1890).

Through painting his "Wheat Field with Crows" he came full circle again. The painting's somber mood is reminiscent of the print that hung in his father's study in Zundert, "Funeral Procession through the Corn Field." The sky looks dark and ominous and a flock of crows fly low over the field. A forked path through a field of high, golden wheat leads to nowhere. But here no church steeple is visible on the horizon. The path is painted in contrasting colors of greens and reds, colors of which Vincent once wrote, *I've tried to express the terrible human passions with the red and the green* (Arles, September 8, 1888). It is another painting where nature and Vincent's own frame of mind coalesced. Corn or wheat remained strong metaphors for life, as Vincent grappled with the joys and sorrows that had always existed side-by-side. But in Auvers, the sorrows were heavy:

> *Do you know what I think about quite often—what I used to tell you long ago, that if I should not succeed, I still thought that what I had worked on would be continued. Not directly, but one is not alone in believing in the things that are true. And what importance do we have personally then? I feel so strongly that the story of people is like the story of wheat, if one is not sown in the earth to germinate there, what does it matter, for one is then milled to become bread.*
>
> *The difference between happiness and unhappiness, both are necessary and useful, and death or disappearance . . . it's so relative, and so is life.*
>
> *Even in the face of an illness that unsettles or makes anxious, this belief is absolutely unshaken.*
>
> —Saint-Rémy, on or about September 20, 1889

The paintings from the last weeks of Vincent's life were created under a lot of stress and burdened with anxiety: about Theo, about their future, about his own health. He painted because that is what kept him from succumbing to despair. He painted "Daubigny's Garden" as an effort to capture a more pleasant scene, an attempt to see the joy beyond his sorrow. *But for one's health, as you say, it is very necessary to work in the garden and to see the flowers growing* (Auvers-sur-Oise, between July 10 and 14, 1890). Yet, in one of the versions of the garden, a black cat and a black figure add a troublingly ominous touch.

Even though he lived in closer proximity to Paris, Vincent suffered from loneliness. The few times he saw Theo and his family did not ease his sense of isolation. The visits were strained because Theo was ill and Johanna, his wife, was exhausted from tending a sick baby. Vincent felt himself to be a burden, knowing that the money Theo sent him was sorely needed for his wife and child. Johanna, in a very loving letter, assured Vincent that he was loved and did not cause them hardships.

In Auvers, Vincent did not find much companionship, and he was often taunted and even ridiculed by village youths, who found him a strange character and a perfect target for their pranks. One of the boys often touted an old pistol. One day in July, Vincent left the inn in his customary way with his easel and paints. He returned without them hours later. Wounded by a bullet in his abdomen he managed to drag himself up to his attic room at the inn. The innkeeper found him lying on his bed and summoned Dr. Gachet and Theo. It is not known what medical care Vincent received, but he never left his bed again. Theo was by his side within hours. The two brothers spent time together in the cramped attic room, talking and sharing a pillow, just as they had in the days of the Zundert parsonage. Vincent died in his brother's arms two days later.

Vincent's painting supplies were never recovered, nor was the weapon that had wounded him. Auvers was a small town. Everyone knew each other. There was no need for an investigation. Dr. Gachet did not have Vincent hospitalized. The local newspaper reported that Vincent had shot himself in the stomach with the intention of killing himself—although he owned no pistol. Because his death was deemed a suicide, the religious authorities and townspeople of Auvers forbade Vincent's body to be buried in the cemetery of the Church of Auvers. He was laid to rest, instead, in the cemetery beyond the walls of the town. Like the "man of sorrow, and acquainted with grief" from the Isaiah passage visible on his Nuenen Bible, Vincent was shunned in life by the established authorities of church and society; why not, also, in death.

At the time of Vincent's burial, the fields of wheat surrounding the cemetery were a ripe golden color, promising a rich harvest.

Bibliography

Source: Vincent's Letters

vangoghletters.org—This is my source for the letters in their original languages, Dutch and French.

The Complete Letters of Vincent van Gogh. 3 volumes. Boston: A Bulfinch Press Book, Little, Brown, Third Edition, 2000.

Vincent van Gogh—The Letters, The Complete Illustrated and Annotated Edition. Amsterdam: Van Gogh Museum, 2009, vangoghletters.org.

A Selection of Books on Vincent van Gogh:

Callow, Philip. *Vincent van Gogh: A Life*. Chicago: Ivan R. Dee Publisher, 1990.

Cabanne, Pierre. *Qui a tue Vincent van Gogh?* Paris: Quai Voltaire, 1992.

Druick, Douglas et al. *Van Gogh and Gauguin: The Studio of the South*. New York: Thames & Hudson, 2001.

Duez, Georges. *Vincent van Gogh au Borinage*. Mons, Belgium: Federation du Tourisme de la Province de Hainaut, 1976.

Erickson, Kathleen Powers. *At Eternity's Gate; The Spiritual Vision of Vincent van Gogh*. Grand Rapids: William B. Eerdmans 1998.

Ford, Cliff. *The Shoes of Van Gogh: A Spiritual and Artistic Journey to the Ordinary*. New York: Crossroad, 2004.

——. *Van Gogh and God: A Creative Spiritual Quest*. Chicago: Loyola Press, 1989.

Helvey, Jennifer. *Irises: Vincent van Gogh in the Garden*. Los Angeles: Getty Publishing, 2009.

Hulsker, Jan. *Van Gogh en zijn weg: Het complete werk*. Amsterdam: Meulenhoff International, 1977.

Huyghe, René. *Van Gogh*. New York: Crown Publishers, 1979.

Kodera, Tsukasa. *Vincent van Gogh: Christianity versus Nature.* Amsterdam: JBPC, 1990.

Lubin, Albert J. *Stranger on the Earth.* London: Paladin, 1975.

Meier-Graefe, Julius. *Vincent van Gogh: A Biographical Study.* New York: Literary Guild of America, New York, 1933.

Naifey, Steven, and Gregory White Smith. *Van Gogh: The Life.* New York: Random House, 2011.

Pierard, Louis. *The Tragic Life of Vincent van Gogh.* London: John Castle, 1925.

Silverman, Debora. *Van Gogh and Gauguin: The Search for Sacred Art.* New York: Farrar, Straus and Giroux, 2000.

Tralbaut. Mark Edo. *Van Gogh: A Pictorial Biography.* New York: Viking Press, 1959.

Wilkie, Ken. *The Van Gogh File: The Myth and the Man.* London: Souvenir Press, 2004.

Other Sources:

Delacroix, Eugene. *The Journal of Eugene Delacroix,* trans. Lucy Norton. London: Phaidon Press, 1951.

Edwards, Betty. *Drawing on the Artist Within.* New York: Simon & Schuster, 1986.

Frank, Frederick. *The Zen of Seeing: Seeing/Drawing as Meditation.* Visalia, CA: Vintage Press, 1973.

Keller, Helen. *The World I Live In*, ed. and with introduction by Robert Shattuck. New York: New York Review of Books 2003.

Authors read by Vincent van Gogh: Charles Dickens, Harriet Beecher Stowe, George Eliot, Victor Hugo, Alphonse Daudet, Edmond and Jules de Goncourt, Émile Zola, Guy de Maupassant, Honoré de Balzac, Charlotte Brontë, Johann Wolfgang von Goethe, John Bunyan, Fyodor Dostoevsky, Gustave Flaubert, Jules Michelet, Leo Tolstoy.

MODERN SPIRITUAL MASTERS

Robert Ellsberg, Series Editor

This series introduces the essential writing and vision of some of the great spiritual teachers of our time. While many of these figures are rooted in long-established traditions of spirituality, others have charted new, untested paths. In each case, however, they have engaged in a spiritual journey shaped by the challenges and concerns of our age. Together with the saints and witnesses of previous centuries, these modern spiritual masters may serve as guides and companions to a new generation of seekers.

Already published:

Modern Spiritual Masters (edited by Robert Ellsberg)
Swami Abhishiktananda (edited by Shirley du Boulay)
Metropolitan Anthony of Sourozh (edited by Gillian Crow)
Eberhard Arnold (edited by Johann Christoph Arnold)
Pedro Arrupe (edited by Kevin F. Burke, S.J.)
Daniel Berrigan (edited by John Dear)
Thomas Berry (edited by Mary EvelynTucker and John Grim)
Dietrich Bonhoeffer (edited by Robert Coles)
Robert McAfee Brown (edited by Paul Crowley)
Dom Helder Camara (edited by Francis McDonagh)
Carlo Carretto (edited by Robert Ellsberg)
G. K. Chesterton (edited by William Griffin)
Joan Chittister (edited by Mary Lou Kownacki and Mary Hembrow Snyder)
Yves Congar (edited by Paul Lakeland)
The Dalai Lama (edited by Thomas A. Forsthoefel)
Alfred Delp, S.J. (introduction by Thomas Merton)
Catherine de Hueck Dogerty (edited by David Meconi, S.J.)
Virgilio Elizondo (edited by Timothy Matovina)
Charles de Foucauld (edited by Robert Ellsberg)
Mohandas Gandhi (edited by John Dear)
Bede Griffiths (edited by Thomas Matus)
Romano Guardini (edited by Robert A. Krieg)
Gustavo Gutiérrez (edited by Daniel G. Groody)

Thich Nhat Hanh (edited by Robert Ellsberg)
Abraham Joshua Heschel (edited by Susannah Heschel)
Etty Hillesum (edited by Annemarie S. Kidder)
Caryll Houselander (edited by Wendy M. Wright)
Pope John XXIII (edited by Jean Maalouf)
Rufus Jones (edited by Kerry Walters)
Clarence Jordan (edited by Joyce Hollyday)
John Main (edited by Laurence Freeman)
Anthony de Mello (edited by William Dych, S.J.)
Thomas Merton (edited by Christine M. Bochen)
John Muir (edited by Tim Flinders)
John Henry Newman (edited by John T. Ford, C.S.C.)
Henri Nouwen (edited by Robert A. Jonas)
Flannery O'Connor (edited by Robert Ellsberg)
Karl Rahner (edited by Philip Endean)
Brother Roger of Taizé (edited by Marcello Fidanzio)
Oscar Romero (by Marie Dennis, Rennie Golden, and Scott Wright)
Albert Schweitzer (edited by James Brabazon)
Frank Sheed and Maisie Ward (edited by David Meconi)
Sadhu Sundar Singh (edited by Charles E. Moore)
Mother Maria Skobtsova (introduction by Jim Forest)
Dorothee Soelle (edited by Dianne L. Oliver)
Edith Stein (edited by John Sullivan, O.C.D.)
David Steindl-Rast (edited by Clare Hallward)
William Stringfellow (edited by Bill Wylie-Kellerman)
Pierre Teilhard de Chardin (edited by Ursula King)
Mother Teresa (edited by Jean Maalouf)
St. Thérèse of Lisieux (edited by Mary Frohlich)
Phyllis Tickle (edited by Jon M. Sweeney)
Henry David Thoreau (edited by Tim Flinders)
Howard Thurman (edited by Mary Krohlich)
Leo Tolstoy (edited by Charles E. Moore)
Evelyn Underhill (edited by Emilie Griffin)
Vincent Van Gogh (by Carol Berry)Jean Vanier (edited by Carolyn Whitney-Brown)
Swami Vivekananda (edited by Victor M. Parachin)
Simone Weil (edited by Eric O. Springsted)
John Howard Yoder (edited by Paul Martens and Jenny Howells)